DANCERS OF GOD

Noël Ballif

Dancers of God

Translated from the French by James Cameron

SIDGWICK AND JACKSON
LONDON

MADE AND PRINTED IN GREAT BRITAIN BY
WILLIAM CLOWES AND SONS, LIMITED, LONDON AND BECCLES

TO MY COMRADES
OF THE
OGOWE-CONGO MISSION

MEMBERS OF THE OGOWE-CONGO MISSION

RAOUL HARTWEG—Professor of Anthropology at the Ethnological Institute of the University of Paris, and in charge of the Expedition's scientific work. He was our senior member, his gifts making him a considerable personality.

GILBERT ROUGET.—Arts graduate, attached to the Musée de l'Homme in Paris. His qualifications as ethnologist and musician made him the man to select the songs and dances for recording.

PIERRE LODS.—Student and ethnologist. He carried his canvases, his brushes and his colours to paint Africa with great artistic freedom.

JACQUES DUPONT.—With his Diploma from the Institute of Cinematographic Studies he took charge of all the filming, and directed our documentaries.

EDMOND SÉCHAN.—"Trotty"—also with a Cinematographic Diploma —was responsible for the actual photography.

PIERRE-DOMINIQUE GAISSEAU.—Speleologist, ex-parachutist, already with some camera experience. He was assistant photographer.

ANDRÉ DIDIER.—Professor at the National Conservatory of Arts and Crafts. He was our sound-technician and engineer, and before we set out he did not hesitate to sell his car so that he could complete his equipment.

GUY NIEF.—Assistant Professor of Physics attached to the National Scientific Research Centre. He assisted Didier with the recording.

FRANCIS MAZIÈRE.—He had the Louvre diploma, and his task was prehistoric research. He made many drawings throughout his journey.

GUY DE BEAUCHÊNE.—A student in the geological laboratory of the Paris Faculty of Science. Besides his geological investigations, he made an important collection of insects.

ERIK HINSCH.—Norwegian student from Oslo University, exhibitioner of the University of Paris. He came to France to complete his archaeological studies. He was the "baby" of the expedition, his good nature getting him adopted by everyone.

6

There is nothing barbarous or savage in this people, from what I learn, save in that all persons call that barbarous which is not of their own experience. Indeed we have no yardstick of truth or of sense other than the example of opinions and methods of our own country—there is always to be found the perfect religion, the perfect police, the perfect and accomplished use of everything.

MONTAIGNE, chap. XXXI

"God gave to every one his own fashions. The parrot does not live like the monkey, nor does the monkey have the customs of the leopard. Thus with men: other men find their way of life in working; as for ourselves, we live on what we can find. That is why we cannot build great villages and cultivate the land. Why? That is not our way."

STATEMENT OF A PYGMY
TO MGR LE ROY

CONTENTS

LIST OF ILLUSTRATIONS

11

Photographs by Noël Ballif and André Didier.

DANCERS OF GOD

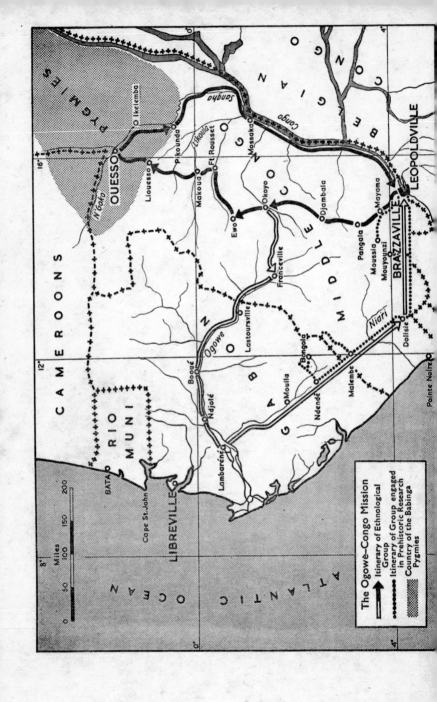

The Ogowé–Congo Mission

→ Itinerary of Ethnological Group
···· Itinerary of Group engaged in Prehistoric Research
▨ Country of the Babinga Pygmies

FORTY CENTURIES . . .

"TO the Heavenly Dancer, greetings. Salutations to him who makes the heart glad, to whom the King Neferkara—may he live for ever—sends homage."

Who was the object of this extraordinary deference? He was a Pygmy. More than four thousand years ago the Egyptian explorer Hirkhouf returned to the royal city of Memphis from a strange journey deep into the Land of Trees, the Country of Spirits, far over the southern borders of the Old Kingdom, bringing with him gifts for the monarch. And the King—one of the last Pharaohs of the Sixth Dynasty—tempered his grandeur with enthusiasm and replied:

"We have noted the letter sent from yourself to the Palace, signalling to Us your return from the Land of Trees. . . . You claim to have brought, among many rich gifts from this Country of Spirits, a Dwarf, so-called a Dancer of God, like unto him whom Ba-Wer-Djed, the Guardian of the Divine Seals, brought also in the day of the King Asosi.

"You inform Us that no Dwarf of such semblance has heretofore been captured by any of those who penetrated the Land of Trees before yourself. Take, then, the northern road forthwith, and bring the Dwarf to Us in Our Palace.

"To the Heavenly Dancer, greetings. Salutations to him who makes the heart glad, to whom the King Neferkara—may he live for ever—sends homage.

15

"When you embark him, post reliable men before and around him, that he fall not into the water. By night, let guardians protect his slumber, watching him ten times through the hours of darkness, as We are eager to see this Dwarf; when you reach Our Palace there must he be beside you, alive and well. We shall provide for you then more richly even than was in his time done for Ba-Wer-Djed, Guardian of the Divine Seals, in the time of the King Asosi; for it is of the greatest moment to Us that We see this Dwarf. Orders have been sent to the officials along your route that provisions be prepared for you at every halt and in every temple. . . ."

More than a thousand years pass by; civilisations sink and others rise; Homer, in the *Iliad*, uses the Pygmy legend as an analogy in his tale of the Trojan War: ". . . the Trojans advance with piercing cries, like a host of birds; thus did the crane-winged people, fleeing from the frosts and floods, bring death and destruction to the race of the Pygmies, letting loose from the skies a terrible war."

In the year 500 B.C. Hanno the Carthaginian vainly attempted the first circumnavigation of Africa; before he turned back he claimed to have seen, on the Gulf of Guinea in what is now the Cameroons, a company of little hairy men with large heads. He gave them the name—in the mistaken belief that he was talking of apes—that became "gorilla".

Some years later Herodotus records the evidence of the Persian Satasque who made a journey similar to that of Hanno, and who also encountered Pygmies on the African coast. He adds furthermore the story of Libyan nomads who penetrated into the unknown

PLATE 1. The Bibaniki dance: outside the ring of dancers, the one who holds the rhythm with an African *marimba*—a long bamboo filled with dried seeds. On his upper lip he carries a strip of soft wood carved into the form of teeth.

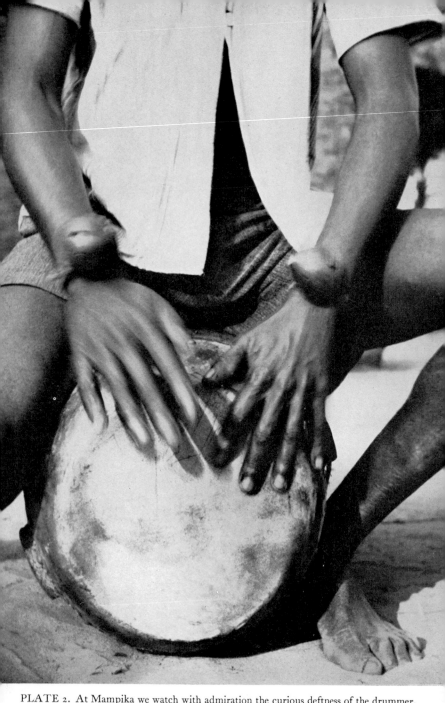

PLATE 2. At Mampika we watch with admiration the curious deftness of the drummer, astride his instrument, his hands and fingers beating out a rapid rhythm.

south. "After several days' travel over the desert they came at last to trees; as they approached to gather fruit they were surprised by little men, far smaller than the ordinary, who took them prisoner and carried them off. They crossed great swamps, and came at length to a town where all who lived were as small as their captors, and as black. Beside the town was a river, flowing from west to east, and peopled with crocodiles."

In the 4th century B.C. Aristotle's *Natural History* says: "In the swamps of the Upper Nile, where the cranes fly from Scythia, there live the Pygmies. This is no legend; it is the truth that there exists a tiny race of both men and horses, living in caves."

Three hundred years later his compatriot Strabo, the geographer, spoke of Pygmies inhabiting the South among the Ethiopians. So did Pliny. One after another the old historians remark the Little People—not only that, but contemporary artists represented their appearance: the Egyptians in bas-relief, among Ethiopian and Libyan captives; the Greeks on their vases. The characteristic Pygmy shape appears on pottery from Cyrenaica and Etruria; the Romans projected it on the frescoes of Herculaneum and Pompeii.

But long before these evidences of the Pygmies were discovered the imagination of mankind had created them for itself, in the form of gnomes and pixies—the elves of Scandinavia, the *korrigans* of Brittany, the German *kobolds* and the Irish leprechauns; a vast and varied assemblage of Little People, either bad or good but always supernatural, always to be encountered by night in the shadow of the trees. These pucks and brownies, however defined, were naturally rejected by those who claimed to be intellectuals; for the same reason they rejected the theory of the African Pygmy. In the

Middle Ages Albert the Great confused them with apes, and they were relegated to simple mythology by the celebrated Italian Renaissance physician Scaliger, the 17th-century German scientist Vossius and the Benedictine savant Dom Augustin Calmet. One investigator after another heard of the Pygmies, examined the evidence and turned them down. Nevertheless, the English sailor Battel—who was captured by the Portuguese in 1589 and who remained nearly eighteen years in the Congo—claimed to have met the Pygmies. Buffon, whose *Natural History* punctuated his time, came to the same conclusion as Albert. His contemporary, the Jesuit François-Xavier de Feller, defined them in his *Historical Dictionary* as "people of Libya, who lived for eight years; their women bore children at five, hiding them in holes so that the cranes, with whom this people was perpetually at war, should not bear them off. . . ." He claimed for the Pygmies the stature of a cubit—about twenty inches—and it is a fact that the Greek word πυγμή means precisely that dimension, and is analogous to the Latin word *pygmaeus*.

Before the end of the 19th century, new explorers had returned with new testimony, and once again the Pygmies took their place definitively among the peoples of Africa. Paul Belloni du Chaillu discovered them in his journeyings to the source of the Ogowe River in 1865. Between July, 1868, and November, 1871, the German naturalist George Schweinfurth crossed the Bahr-el-Gazal marshes to the banks of the Ouellé, a Congo tributary. At the court of King Mounza of the Mombutu he, too, found Pygmies—the Akka people, whom the Egyptians had known four thousand years before and whose image the Egyptologist Mariette had found on the bas-reliefs of Beni-Hassan.

Furthermore the anthropologist Quatrefages de Bréau recorded: "It is clear that in spite of their small stature, their comparatively long arms, their short legs and exaggerated bellies, the Akka are authentic men, and those who have considered them as semi-apes are thoroughly confounded today."

One by one, as they penetrated the equatorial forest, the new explorers met more Pygmies. Stanley himself, returning after his famous East-West crossing of Africa to the neighbourhood between Lake Albert and the Congo, wrote: "It was here I saw the first member of the dwarf tribe, which was said to have been completely dispersed to the north of the Itouri. . . . She measured scarcely a yard high; she was a perfectly formed young woman, some seventeen years old. Her skin was glossy and fair. Her silhouette was that of a coloured woman in miniature, not without a certain grace, and her face was very prepossessing. Her colour was that of a quadroon, or of pale ivory. Her eyes were magnificent, but abnormally large for such a small creature—almost as large as those of a young gazelle—wide, prominent, and extremely brilliant. Absolutely naked, the little lady was wholly sure of herself, as though she were accustomed to being admired."

Monseigneur Le Roy, who often studied the Pygmies of the Gabon, relates from the lips of Pierre Savorgnan de Brazza his first encounter with the Little People when he entertained a tribe on the banks of the Likouala, tributary of the Congo: "Who are these people? What—you do not know them? They are the ones who invented fire . . ."

So many travellers, explorers, anthropologists encountered the Pygmies in the forests which extend from the Atlantic coast to the Great Lakes, yet no significant expedition ever succeeded in living in any sort of proximity to their villages.

When I was studying at the Ethnological Institute of the University of Paris I was secretary of the Louis Liotard Group of the Explorers' Club—named after a member assassinated in 1940 in Tibet. The object of this group was to unite young men anxious to develop whatever were their scientific or technical specialities in overseas travel. It was my wish to go with Hartweg and Rouget to the country of the Babinga Pygmies in the Central Congo. We chose this part of the French Union firstly because the best chance existed there of finding the people we were seeking; also because there we might receive official support, and we were by no means rich.

Backed by the Musée de l'Homme, we began to make up our party: I had always wanted to take with me a team of cinema technicians to make sure of the sort of film and sound recordings that would not only be indispensable for our research, but which would in themselves be of intrinsic interest. The expedition was rounded off with a painter, two archaeologists and a geologist. Under the patronage of M. Achille Urbain, Director of the National Museum of Natural History, and by the Ministry of National Education, we became the "Ogowe-Congo Mission of the Ministry of France Overseas."

We had promises of all facilities for our movements in the territories of Central Congo and the Gabon. The problem of our transport from Paris to Brazzaville was solved by General Bouscat, Chief of Staff of the Air Force, who offered to take us by one of the military aircraft which at that time maintained regular contact between French Equatorial Africa and France. It was then necessary to find a producer interested in the documentary film proposition. Eight days before we were due to leave, after many disappointments, Dupont and Didier met M. Lemaire and M. Schlitz, of the Société d'Applications Cinématographiques, who had enough confidence in us to provide us with cameras, film and recording gear. Thus after six months of tireless effort the twelve of us managed to assemble ourselves and our resources, ready to depart.

As I reached for my traveller's hat I consciously tried to put away the habits and prejudices of a lifetime, so that I might the better get to know these remote people who would share with me the joys and sorrows of human beings.

Chapter I

*Into the Interior – Encounter with the Ants – The
Difficult Roads – Fertility Dances – The African
Ballet.*

I SAT beside Samba the driver, with his beret and his
glinting, rakish eyes, and I stared through the window
as Brazzaville slipped behind us. The city has no
suburbs; as soon as you leave the tarred road for the
earth track you are threading through the empty
country, through a tumbled region of hills that somehow recalls Auvergne, except that here the pasture is
scorched to the colour of rust and the little streams
trickle through valleys dense with vegetation, with contending bamboo groves and palm. We rolled over a
wooden bridge—a man bore on his head a mound of
bananas; two women walked behind him, their infants
on their backs. The villages grew rarer, the distances
between them longer. Already the road was soft with
sand. The car slowed down; the wheels thrust and
slipped through the loose surface.

There had been two long weeks in Brazzaville col-
lecting our gear and, above all, rounding up the transport that the Administration had promised us. Every
day the film men stared despairingly at the sky—
leaden, solid. We thought of the thirty thousand feet of
film we had brought with us. Jacques and André had
briefed themselves with information from the Meteoro-
logical Department: south of the Equator, they said,

there was no use counting on good cinematic conditions before October, when the rains came. That was the paradox: only the daily storms would break up that sullen sky.

We were going north. We had decided to make for Ouesso, some four hundred and fifty miles from Brazzaville, on the map. From there we would reach the forest where we hoped to find a Pygmy camp. Our plan was to stay there a few weeks, to do what ethnological and anthropological researches we could, to study and record the music. When that work was done we would go to the Gabon, and make another documentary of the Ogowe rapids from Franceville to Lambaréné.

The archaeologists had mapped out a programme that began with a study of the geological formations around Brazzaville, in the neighbourhood of Mayama and Pangala, and continued with an intensive three-month investigation of the Nyari and Nyanga valleys.

When we were sufficiently furnished with contradictory information we made out a project-report for the Government. The Ministry in Paris had announced us in advance as a scientific mission; I think the local Administration had expected a body of dignified professors, and we were all disappointingly young. Nevertheless, after we had paid several calls and explained our plans, we got our official help—clothes and shoes, tents and mess-kits, guns and ammunition from the Army; provisions from the commissariat; and a useful medical kit from the Health Department that was to be used on whoever might need it on our travels, as well as on ourselves. In the original planning in Paris I had decided to ask for our subsidy to be provided in kind, like this, rather than in a cash subvention, arguing that we should find what we needed better on the spot.

We tested and checked the equipment; divided the stock of film and discs into half which we should carry with us and half for the second expedition down the Ogowe which we should pick up later. We divided the supplies similarly: the flour, the rice, the salt, the tins of condensed milk, the jam, the tea and coffee, sugar and oil, and the precious bottles of brandy which were the only luxury on the list. Furthermore, we each carried a canvas bag containing a blanket, two sheets, a light mattress, a mosquito-net and a folding bed. We made up two sets of cooking gear—our individual plates and cutlery, two saucepans, two frying-pans and a coffee-mill. We kept two tents and left one for the archaeologists.

The days went by. We were ready, but our two lorries were not; they were still under repair. We had already embarked a good deal of our gear on the little steamer *Balin*, which was going to Ouesso by way of the Congo and the Sangha.

Jacques and Trotty, Rouget and Didier would go ahead in one truck, taking Pierre, the cook; we should catch them up on the northern track, at Djambala. They would take two cameras, the Arriflex and the Eyemo, and the recording machinery, on the chance that they might get some work done on the road.

Our final task was to thank M. Soucadaux the Secretary-General, General Duchaussoy, Commander of the Army of French Equatorial Africa, and the other officials who had helped us. At last the transport was ready; we were off.

In the worst places the sand was overlaid with a dense matting of heavy, dry grass from the neighbouring slopes. In enormous clouds thrown up by the wheels we rolled along on a kind of immense mattress. At midday the sun beat down like a blow. I offered my seat to anyone who preferred the stifling heat of the cabin to the suffocating dust-bath of the open lorry.

At the top of a long slope we made a halt beside a market—a simple stockade of wooden rails. It was already late in the day, but there was still a crowd, selling tiny eggs, small and bony chickens, roots of manioc and lengths of sugar-cane. Our arrival caused a sensation. The headman of the local village, armed with an umbrella, brought his hand to a splendid black felt hat in an exaggerated salute. He ceremoniously offered us a calabash of some milky liquid. We could not refuse it —slightly acid, faintly sparkling, very refreshing; it was palm-wine. We passed the calabash from mouth to mouth and handed it back to its owner, who finished it in one gulp and asked us very civilly if we could drop him and two friends some way up the road. We invited them on board, all three of them, complete with bags of victuals and a pair of indignantly protesting ducks.

The sand-track gave way to a good laterite road. Thick swirls of red dust trailed behind us; we began to take on an overall brick colour. Crossing the M'Fia by the ferry, we came to Mayama.

Early next morning, before we left, the postman brought a telegram from Didier: "Road very bad between Pangala-Djambala. Numerous sand-drifts. Make sure of breakdown kit. See you at Djambala."

Under a grey sky the two lorries—ours and the archaeologists'—moved along; theirs at a respectful distance, since behind each truck lay five hundred yards of the dust-storm. It was a good road, and we soon made the crossroads where we were to separate, for they were making for the Kindemba mission to explore a series of grottoes that had already been recorded by M. Bergeaud in 1938. We wished each other a brief good-bye and good luck, and our ways divided.

Seven or eight times during that afternoon we were held up by the slack, resisting sand. Each time it was necessary to get out, to push and to pull, to lay planks below the whirling tyres. In the most troublesome places it was necessary to do even more; we had to unload the boxes and the canteens; somehow or other we contrived to get through. Then, in the valley of the Léfini, with the forest only a few miles ahead, the heavy truck slid to a stop. We had taken an hour to move eight hundred yards, leaving behind us a trail of tremendous holes. Now we were truly stuck—we tested the road ahead; it was soft and hopeless. Samba decided that the only possible expedient would be to leave the track and ride over the verge, where the sand seemed to be solidified by the tufts and hummocks.

Once again we went through the dismal business of unloading, and tried again. The only answer to this surface problem, it seemed, would be speed and momentum. The lorry bucked and rolled along the verge, and we were over. There was no more to do but walk back and carry across the cargo. We were on the point of moving off when Samba, looking up from his inspection, said, "The main leaf of the spring is broken in two places."

There was no question of continuing along this dreadful road without a repair. Night was falling and a village was near at hand. We edged the lorry gently towards it. At Mampika we were quickly adopted. As we sat beside the fire I became full of admiration for a boy whose extraordinarily nimble hands and fingers beat out a complex rhythm on his drum; a rattle on his wrists shook out a brittle shower of sound against the rumble of the tomtom. A baby played with a dog. We had set up the tent nearby, under a thick palm. Hartweg, who had been wandering among the huts, suddenly came back triumphantly with three pineapples, gave me a mysterious look and said:

"There are Pygmies here. I have just seen a little shack in a corner. Come and see."

He led me through the shadows to a little building scarcely bigger than a beehive, full of gentle stirring sounds. The hen-house (which is what it in fact was) had been built on stilts two feet off the ground, to protect the chickens from the predatory small game of the forest.

Pierre and I sauntered out in the milky moonlight, a strange pearly luminosity shining through the mist on the tall grass and the darkling trees. There was the kind of silence in which one shrinks from speech. Both of us jumped as some bird broke the stillness with a wild, long-drawn call, blundered heavily overhead and disappeared.

Just before the trees we halted in front of a narrow fissure some six inches wide which crossed the track, dividing into two branches on the left. I knelt to examine the strange sight: there in the moonlight slowly trickled a ribbon of blood. Pierre began to strike matches. Without taking my eyes from this bizarre thread of movement I touched it with the toe of my sandal—and instantly cried out; I felt the bites through my woollen socks. I pulled away five or six half-inch ants, which hung on desperately. The moving trail of blood was a column of brown ants; we stared at them in the match-light—on they moved, uninterrupted, undistracted. With a twig we drove them from their marching order—it made no difference; automatically each insect rejoined the column, and continued its remorseless journey. On each side the regiment was protected by a flanking cordon of black ants; it was those which had bitten me. The sentries waited there, sparring on their back legs, vigilant and ready for any attack. In some places, built one upon the other, they formed a kind of suspension-bridge over the packed and plodding battalions.

The moon broke out, suddenly intense, outlining the forest silhouette, gleaming on the fast-flowing river. Pierre and I left this sinister army of ants and sat on the bank to smoke a cigarette. Then suddenly, as we were about to return, there came the sound of a far-away motor on the other side of the Léfini. It drew nearer. Who could be driving on that empty trail through the darkness of Africa? The beams of headlights swung brutally across the river and a lorry stopped; there came the sound of voices. I recognised the tones of Jacques and Rouget. They were rousing the ferryman who slept in one of the steel boats that supported the ferry's landing. He brought them slowly across the river. They had come to help us over the bad patch of road, where they themselves would still have been stranded if reinforcements had not arrived, sent by the Administrator at Djambala. They had made use of their time by filming and recording a burial ceremony on the Koukouya plateau.

At daybreak Samba and the newcomers managed to finish our repairs. We shifted some of our load over to the newly-arrived truck, and Jacques showed me what he claimed was his completely successful device for overcoming the sand-drifts. It was a set of heavy mats of basketwork, some two yards by one: a solid platform for the spinning wheels. We provided our truck with a set; the sun appeared in the sky; one after the other our trucks set off on another day.

Immediately across the river we left the valley for a completely desolate plateau, treeless, dusted with a thin, dry grass. For the first few miles the road was hard, but soon the sand appeared again, and here the soft beds were no longer matted with the tangled grass. The other truck was already stuck in front of us and, sooner than risk this, Samba edged off the road and ground over a carpet of ashes, where the bush had been burned by the Africans.

As we drew ahead of our friends we, too, floundered to a stop; the back wheels spun in a whirlwind of sand and buried themselves. Samba switched off the engine; there was no point in insisting on the impossible. We flattened the sand in front of the wheels, laid down our mats—the engine roared, the tyres ground and bit into the basketwork; clumsily and resentfully the truck advanced on the reedy platform as we ran beside the wheels, lifting the mats, replacing them. And after another fifty yards we were able to leap on to the running-board as the ground solidified underneath us.

The other truck passed us in its turn; it drove squarely by, outside the track, and there was no more for us to do than follow over the white sand, under the dark sky.

The road—one could still describe it as a road—bent down into a valley, suddenly cheered with a ray of sunlight. There lay the M'Pama, banked with constellations of butterflies, great lazy multitudes which moved only when immediately threatened, yet somehow wan and lustreless. The water was tepid—here, said the ferrymen, there were no crocodiles, and so we bathed; as the ferry plodded across we played in the lukewarm water. Once out of the river it was important to seize branches to drive off the great particoloured flies, the black-and-orange tsetse whose bite bears the sleeping-sickness.

For hours, then, the pickup led us through an empty land. From time to time the motor would cough, hesitate, and stop. Ignace, the driver, would brake the truck, get out, open the bonnet, go through a meticulous examination of the plugs, the wiring, the carburettor, all with a scrupulous and wholly normal air. Then Didier would do something to the feed-pump and the engine would cough itself into action. Five hundred yards farther on, the routine would begin again. The lorry caught us up; everyone would gather round to watch Didier repeat the performance.

Now this calcined earth was brushed with new grass, decorated curiously with the towers and gables of little yard-high ant-hills. Towards the east a rolling mountain of clouds climbed above the low wall of the forest, as though already the storms were building; long spears of the dying sunlight cut through the blankets of mist. Here was the vast emptiness of Africa, an infinite desolation; not a human being, not a living beast, not even the song of a bird—nothing alive but the uncountable, teeming insects for ever humming around our heads.

Each new delay was especially irksome, but there is

31

nothing to be gained by chafing against the caprices of engineering. The last hold-up turned out to be really serious, and into a depressed hush Didier dropped his diagnosis: now it was the petrol feed which was out of action; there was no chance of an on-the-spot repair. We should have to go to Okoyo.

Didier took charge of the operation, and in the failing minutes of the daylight we created a strange piece of apparatus. I sat on the cabin roof, firmly gripped by Dupont, and leaned forward with a rubber tube, one end of which was stuck into a petrol-can held by Dominique on the bonnet. Didier, prone on the mud-guard, held the other end of the tube above the carburettor, observing the drips of petrol and reflecting on the imminent danger of fire. Trotty stood by with the fire-extinguisher.

Ignace took the wheel. Didier controlled the petrol drop by drop. The engine coughed, hesitated—and began to turn. With this strange team disposed in its peculiar action-stations the pickup began, very slowly, to move. Happily the track was not too bad, for we had another thirteen miles between us and Okoyo, and already the night had dropped over us. So we groped our way along yard by yard, with the headlamps of the lorry behind us outlining the extraordinary shadows of this man-machine pyramid; the track rose and fell beside a coppice stirring with the rustling of questing animals.

At last we came to the Alima—a ferry veiled in a haze of whining mosquitoes, on the other bank the dark forms of huts: Okoyo.

The early sun flooded down on a patch of sand where the poultry scratched and gossiped. We awoke re-

32

PLATE 3. Esakatoumbo, the ballet-master.

PLATE 4. The "Mass"—with Yénégué holding aloft a chaplet of dried seeds before the kneeling Bibaniki.

freshed, and demanding only one thing, a bath, went down to the river. Here, less than sixty miles from its source, the Alima is only some thirty yards wide, a clear stream between tree-banked shores. We soaped on the bank, dived in from the landing. The Africans were washing all around us. They stripped and then, with a curious adroit modesty, they cupped their hand over their sex as they stood on the shore. Two old women waited chatting nearby. One of them, on her knees, was washing clothes in a little creek, already creamed with suds; the other soaped a baby, then immersed it deep in the water, gripping it by the arm. With each ducking the little boy sneezed and laughed.

Didier toiled away in the shade of the tall palms. He had taken down the petrol pump and was assembling a new joint. He had brought with him everything he might need for just such a job; without Didier's foresight and resource we might have been endlessly immobilised in Okoyo. We were more than two hundred and seventy miles from any garage. But by the morning's end the motor turned, and continued to turn.

Okoyo to Ewo: sixty miles of changeless countryside, a plain of brittle grass and underbrush, occasional glens and corridors of trees, infrequent villages where we could not stop. When we arrived, it was night once more.

M. Barbereau, the Administrator of the subdivision, and his wife had been waiting for us three days, and so had the patient dancers and singers who had been rounded up from the neighbourhood, for the sake of our cameras and recordings. The dancing was to be done in a broad arena bordered with mango-trees and divided by an alley of palms. As Jacques set up his camera under a copse we heard the singing begin.

They were men and women and children, people of the M'Béti. They wore strips of white cotton round the loins, and as they moved they surrounded two mummers identically dressed in an intricate costume of raffia banded round the body; they had a strikingly inconsequential look of Michelin men. Their masks were painted in white and ochre with the eyes and nose outlined in black; they overtopped the heads around them by two feet, and were certainly carried in some fashion high above the wearers' shoulders.

Dominique had set up the lights, Trotty filmed; the company moved in to within a few yards and the maskbearers placed themselves with the musicians in the centre. The orchestra, of three drums and a wind instrument, gave rhythm to the singers, who chanted a simple recitative, with repeating phrases from the whole group.

This was "Linguéké", a fertility-dance. It is performed at the birth of twins—represented here by the two masks. From time to time a woman emerged from the circle and approached one of the mummers, offering her belly, which she agitated violently. The maskbearer strutted a moment, then, with a bound, whirled on himself, brandishing his huge straw arms. One young girl, apple-breasted, clad in a *cache-sexe* and a swinging necklace, allowed herself readily to be photographed as she danced, invoking the goodwill of the spirits.

For a while the cameramen gave way to the sound crew. We had a transformer delivering 110 volts of alternating current from an accumulator; it seemed to work. Nief dangled his microphone over the dancers at the end of an improvised bamboo sound-boom. After an hour of this performance we had filmed and recorded what seemed to us a useful proportion of the show, but

34

more dancers and musicians were waiting impatiently to put on their acts. I was not particularly keen on these over-produced and organised performances, but we had to make use of the occasion; after all, nothing of the kind had ever been photographed in the region before.

Before he packed up the gear Didier produced his surprise for the crowds milling around the instruments, and played back one of the acts he had just recorded. The effect was superb. At first the astonished singers listened in a profound silence to the sound of their own voices; then they began to smile; little by little they took up the air again, with laughter and little cries of delight.

The sun climbed to the roof of the sky; we moved over to the Administrator's house. But a sudden clamour arose, and a new group of some fifty men advanced upon us. They wore only a fibrous loincloth or a brief ribbon, but they were daubed from head to foot with a white or ochre base and loud stripes and patterns in contrasting colours. They wore on their heads or on their backs—or indeed on both at once—tremendous bunches of plumes sometimes a yard across, great tufts of bustard feathers, black, with a white topknot at the summit in blue or yellow. Among them we noticed a boy of some ten to twelve years old, wearing a miniature head-dress.

By now it was nearly five and the light was failing. Jacques asked Didier to take the Eyemo camera, while Trotty kept the Arriflex; the two cameras were useful to make sure of big groupings and longshots.

M. Barbereau stopped by with his secretary to watch us at work. The secretary was an African in a khaki suit, helmeted—he seemed the characteristic *évolué*, with a just-detectable scorn for all the surrounding capers that somehow suggested the patronising dignity of a Parisian tourist at a country fair. I went up and asked them questions about the dancers.

"They are the Batéké. They come from several villages hereabouts. We call them 'the bandits'."

"The bandits? Why?"

"I don't know. My predecessor called them that. I dare say the first Administrator here gave them the name—anyhow, it has stuck ever since."

"But what do they call themselves?"

"They are the Bibaniki," said the secretary, and that was all I could find out. By now the dancers had gathered round a pole, carried by one of the dancers, decorated with a bird's beak, some raffia bows and a little woven bag filled with white feathers. All the Bibaniki were assembled in concentric circles around the musicians, who themselves surrounded the pole. To a rapid rhythm, and with the motion of people running very fast in the same place, they began to shuffle out each for himself a hole in the sand. They were accompanied by the orchestra, banging with pieces of wood on big, roughly-forged gongs and blowing into huge calabashes.

It was an intensely vigorous yet wholly static ballet. The pace accelerated, the dancers' legs dug themselves into the soft sand up to the calf; little whirling clouds surrounded them. Trotty began filming hard; in ten more minutes the light would be gone, and already the shadows stretched long and fantastic across the ground. Still the dancers shuffled and dug; by now several of them were knee-deep.

When filming was impossible we stopped the dancers in their extraordinary performance.

"A good thing too," said M. Barbereau; "once they

get going they can keep it up for hours. I once saw some of them get down as far as their shoulders."

Esakatoumbo—the dance-master, who was also the village headman—came up to me; he wanted to be photographed. He was the essence of decorum. He wore a string waistcoat hung with coins and an old medal, and round his neck a whistle. On his head was a sort of leather uniform-hat with a white feather. The oddest article of his costume was a great pair of spectacles: two great circles of black flecked with red dots; they engulfed half his face and quite concealed his eyes. Behind this vaguely sinister façade was an expression of gentle placidity.

Didier played us back two more songs. The first was "Ongoukadjoko", a kind of dialogue between Yénégué, the chorus-master, and the Bibaniki. Whether this represents a sequence of praise for the two masters of ceremony or for two chiefs it is hard to say, since it is in some way both at once:

Yénégué: "You who are always the first,
      Take the first place."
Chorus: "Take it.
      Drums, sound your loud tongues.
      Take it."
Yénégué: "Only the spokesman speaks."
Chorus: "What do you say? What do you say?"
Yénégué: "The drum is for me alone.
      Hé, hé, hé."

The second song was an invitation to the dance when one among the dancers must die:

Yénégué: "The little fish."
Chorus: "He's dead, he's dead, he's dead.
      Oh dji dji."

37

Yénégué (after a pause): "Quiet!"
Chorus: "We are quiet."
Yénégué: "The ant begins to tremble."
Chorus: "Tremble, tremble."
Chorus (after a pause): "Good-day!"

The curious last word shares the two meanings of "awakening" and "resurrection".

The Bibaniki had saved a surprise for us before we left. The recording gear was already packed in the pickup, and there was no question of exposing another inch of film. The dancers had dispersed, the women had retreated to their cooking pots. There was nothing left of the performance except the pattern of holes in the sand.

Then we saw that the dancers were, in fact, all kneeling in a long column with Yénégué, upright, a few yards in front of them. In a suddenly powerful voice he cried that he was going to "celebrate a Mass". A murmur ran through the kneeling men. The "priest" had a rosary of huge beads in his hand. He lifted his arms high and recited some incomprehensible formula, turned to the congregation and administered a blessing with a vague but vast sign of the Cross. The assemblage murmured some response, imitated a series of symbolic gestures made by Yénégué, all with a deep, unsmiling seriousness.

This parody took me by surprise. At no time was it the grotesque caricature that a burlesque of the Catholic office can be when performed by those who have in fact practised it piously at one time. On the contrary, the Bibaniki seemed in some way responsive to the mystery of the rite; it was as though they attempted to derive from this imitation some part of the secret power associated with the ritual. The whole thing lasted a bare six minutes; then the company rose to its feet and slipped away among the trees.

M. Barbereau said he had never seen such a thing performed before.

Next morning, while the others loaded the trucks, I talked to a young man who had offered the night before to straighten out my information on the Bibaniki—a man named Gregory, who spoke good French.

To begin with, he said, the name "bandits" was meaningless. The truth was that the Bibaniki formed a community of which each member was in the service of the group; they inhabited several villages, under the control of headmen, and they could be required to help, for example, in ridding the neighbourhood of a troublesome animal, possibly a panther. Outside these occasions they met generally at the death of one of the tribe to divide among themselves his personal effects. Gregory had been the previous year to the funeral of a man whose child it was that we had seen among the dancers last night and who had taken his father's place.

Now the transport was about to move. The lorry came down in front of the post-office, turning towards the road for Fort Rousset, a hundred miles away. The pickup followed behind and Rouget hailed me—I had to leave Gregory and his story; there had been just time to half-open the door leading to an unknown land.

Chapter II

The Drummers of Oando – Welcome on the Equator – The Fish Women – The Dangerous Bridge – Cries in the Night.

AHEAD lay the Equator, somewhere under the lowering sky and the black and mountainous clouds. The earth road was good, driving between banks of high grass, broken here and there with brushwood, or an occasional tall tree. Now we were on the final spurs of the Batéké ridge; the valleys waited before us: the tributaries of the Congo, the Likouala and the Sangha. The great rain-forest was drawing near.

Once we had to run the gauntlet of a minor but rather exciting forest fire, forcing our way through the embers while long flames licked the tree-trunks with a harsh crackling, and an acrid smoke curled thick ribbons round the branches. We were concerned mainly about the fifteen thousand feet of film and the records, all intensely inflammable. It was important to see that the truck did not fail us again at this point. The lorry jumped forward, with Jacques and Dominique beating the top cover to see it had no time to catch fire. The little truck came immediately on our tail, and we were through. These forest fires are fairly commonplace; it is the villagers' way of clearing a new space for cultivation.

Now the track was a morass. From Ewo to Fort Rousset the road followed the Kouyou, which overflowed at intervals, and it was a whole day's work to cover eighty miles—plenty of time to reflect on how tremendously this problem of transport and communications affects the whole development of the country. Until some system of decent roads replaces these tracks of alternating sand and mud the Middle Congo —a territory four-fifths the size of France—is bound to remain a backward place.

After dinner we went to Oando, a little Kouyou village a mile and a half from Fort Rousset, set under a misty moon. We were met by a mob of inquisitive and merry urchins; their parents had already shut themselves in the huts. We were looking for musicians, but all we could find was a couple of young men in shorts and vests with drums—yes, they said casually, they played them from time to time. . . . Rouget decided not to bother with a recording there. One of the lads drifted off, the other stayed, seemingly happy to chat. By and by he began almost absently to hum a vague song, and his fingers caressed the tight skin of his drum in a gentle accompaniment; it gave out a deeper, more hollow reverberation than the usual drum note. It was about a foot across, and a good yard high. Dominique, squatting across the other drum, began to experiment. The little boys gathered around, laughing, but the young man seemed genuinely glad to have interested us in something that he completely understood. He showed how to relax the wrist, to drop the hand freely on the drumhead . . . when the rhythm came, he followed it without thought, submitting his senses one by one to its needs, until the body and all its muscles abandoned themselves to the demands of the tempo, the splendid thud and murmur of the palms on the drum, the ripple of the fingers; he was playing on his own heart; the music was held within this closed circuit:

from the mind to the hands and back to the mind. Why should one ever stop?

I tried to do it myself: as the rhythmic pattern became clearer to me I had the slightest foretaste of that curious interior satisfaction, that fulfilment somewhere outside space and time that the great drummers must know.

Before leaving Fort Rousset we had a long talk with Father Desfosses, a travelling missionary who was in the neighbourhood for the Assumption. Yes, he had met the Pygmies, but—his little eyes glinted behind his spectacles—he would not conceal from us that in his opinion we had just about no chance at all of spending any time in one of their camps. However, if one was able to get near them—we could try, it was a matter of luck. We should not be able to forecast their movements nor the routes they would take; they kept all their plans very secret, said the priest. Still—we should establish ourselves at Matadi, where the river boats refuelled with wood; around there the Babinga had occasionally made contact with white men; it was possible they might be less shy. On the other hand—he shook his head—the fact of their having had those contacts might have made them even more elusive. He wished us luck; it was clear he had no great hopes.

We moved off finally through the broad savannah broken with patches of forest, along a road that at last showed life, with many villages and well-made huts in rows among the palms. As we passed the Kouyou rose and waved a pleasant greeting.

At dusk, there was the Equator. And there, resting precisely on 0° of longitude, the village of Ebala. Our welcome there was astonishing, almost delirious; we rolled into town followed by clamorous crowds. Why the sensation? Ebala, it seemed, was the native village of Joachim, our cook-boy, who had been dropped here by the lorry ahead. Intensely proud of his part in our expedition, he had spread the word of our extraordinary activities: our cameras, our recorders, the strange interest we took in simple things like singing and dancing. The word had gone round every corner of the village, and when the truck came to a stop we were several minutes shaking the hands that reached out from everywhere. There, in the crowd, was Joachim. He laughed aloud when we arranged the rendezvous with him: next day, in Makoua, on the banks of the river.

We sat with glasses of whisky in our hands in the dining-room of M. Bernard, the district Health Officer, surrounded by his big family. That morning, M. Bernard had promised, we should see the leper village he had made himself and where he gave treatment every day.

We had gone only a few yards down a narrow pathway buried in the brush when we heard singing. About a dozen men had gathered in the open space around the sick quarters and the whitewashed surgery. From the grey sky fell a curious light, diffuse but clear. The lepers, in spite of their grim disfigurements, their ruined faces, their decayed and mutilated limbs, had decided to welcome us with music. We did not set up the camera gear right away; for a while we listened to their song.

Later, while the work of filming and recording went on, I sat idly on the surgery verandah. As I waited I saw a woman nearby, engaged in some strange process;

it was as though she were making up for some bizarre purpose. She sat on a mat and arranged before her the contents of a little basket: leaves filled with powders, white and ochre and black, which she mixed with water into a paste. In this she dipped a three-pointed instrument made of feathers tied together and, with very great care, drew on her face parallel coloured lines. For a while I stared at her without daring to interrupt, then I moved over and asked a male nurse what this meant. He was busy; he merely said: "She's an Ikéké. Malarial. She is here for observation." He pointed out a leper who would interpret for me, and we moved over and sat beside the woman. Without the slightest sign of surprise or embarrassment she continued to paint herself as though we did not even exist. We waited until she had finished, and I asked a few hesitant questions.

It seemed that the Ikéké is a fish, no larger than a hand, which is caught in baskets by the women from the edge of the rivers. It has a red mouth, and on its silver-grey sides are vertical lines, red, white and black —exactly like those which the woman was so painstakingly painting on her own face, arms, and breast. Whenever at the birth of a girl in the region one of the old women distinguishes on the infant's face a suggestion of parallel markings, the child is declared an Ikéké, and whatever her future—married, unmarried, widowed—she will remain an Ikéké until the end of her life. Frequently the mother is also Ikéké, but this is not necessary or usual. The birth of an Ikéké, like her death, is always celebrated by all the other Ikéké of the neighbourhood with music and dancing—but the drums must be played by small boys since men, even if they are married to an Ikéké, may take no part in their ceremonies.

The Ikéké have a local priestess, the Omenga. This woman is in charge of the songs and dances, organises the feasts and ceremonies of the sisterhood.

One dietary regulation is strictly enforced: no Ikéké woman may ever eat the Ikéké fish, although they are allowed to catch it.

When an Ikéké falls ill she is isolated in her hut for anything from six to twelve months, depending on her station in life. Her husband, relatives, friends have to buy from the Omenga permission to visit her, since only the Omenga has the authority to open the Ikéké's hut, and the Omenga charges for her ministration. If the Omenga herself becomes ill, only other Omenga from different districts, and the local Ikéké, can nurse her.

This Ikéké, a Kouyou called M'Boualé, talked openly and without hesitation. She herself was an Omenga of a year's standing, and that justified the ritual marks she was painting on her body. She was very frank about it. "I wanted to become an Omenga," she said, "because I have been an Ikéké long enough, and paid the Omenga for looking after me long enough. Now it's my turn."

She explained the details of her initiation. First the postulant consults the village Omenga, and then remains enclosed in her hut for a year. She is left alone, lying on her bed-mat. If she wishes to rise to her feet she must take care to walk on another mat, for during the whole period of seclusion her feet must never touch the earth. She may have no sexual relations with her husband without the Omenga's permission, nor must he even see her without authority.

M'Boualé's novitiate was intensely restricted. Her daughter prepared her food and cleaned the hut; her mother prepared her daily bath. No one could call on

45

her; neither could she leave her hut, nor be seen out of doors. In the event of some catastrophe or wholly unforeseen emergency—if, for example, the village were evacuated by the Administration for some reason—she could still leave her hut only with her feet shod, with a matting cowl over her head, and with her eyes modestly lowered. This isolation could last for years, indeed for as long as it took the woman's family to raise the fee necessary for her graduation. It has happened that some Ikéké have become so etiolated, like a plant deprived of sunlight, that they have died as a result.

I asked one more question about this strange cosmetic process of the Ikéké, and she said: yes, she applied the curious paint-marks once a day before she took food, abstaining only on the days of fasting. Then I got up, thanked the interpreter, and left M'Boualé, the new Omenga, to her dinner.

The night dripped down in a procession of hot and humid hours; in the dense and suffocating damp warmth there could be no sleep. The silence built itself in layers upon the restless brain, a growing multiplication of emptiness that seemed poised for some sort of interruption. Then it came: one by one, in a sort of hurried insistence, the heavy drops of rain began drumming on the corrugated iron above, and at last the sky opened itself with a sort of clamorous relief—the rains had come. Once come, it seemed that the natural inhibitions dissolved: the sky cracked open and a new wind whipped aside the tumbling clouds and tore them into shreds. As an abrupt squall shook the huts Rouget got up, reeled sleepily over to secure the stores. I grunted an acknowledgement and turned over. Outside the hut the rain thudded down in cataracts.

We crossed the Kouyou by the ferry. By now the jungle had replaced the brushwood; from henceforth the track was to be no longer shifting sand, but clinging mud. The night's storm had left broad pools reflecting the drifting image of the broken clouds; around us lay the tattered, amputated leaves of the cotton-tree. The great trunks rose among a confusion of tendrils and lianas crawling one on another, trying but never managing to reach the upper branches, fifty yards overhead. Below contended the palms, the arecas with their slender fingers topped with a bunch of feathery leaves. Here and there a cotton-tree stood up like an immense pillar, stretching a sheltering canopy of foliage over all else. There was something sombre, almost grim, about it that day, under a sky still charged with menace. I grew weary of an endless contemplation of an unchanging corridor of green; I laid my head on a pile of blankets and slept.

The little truck, ahead of us by some minutes, was to wait for us after the Mabili crossing. After ten minutes on the other side, Jacques grew impatient and decided to go on. But five minutes later he paused again—fifteen minutes dragged by, and by now they were worried enough to turn back. As they neared the river an African appeared, shouting: "The lorry's fallen into the water—it's finished!"

Arriving on the bank, they could see the ferry, in mid-stream, on a waterway heavily flooded and adrift with the debris of trees. There was a simultaneous thought: the truck had gone over the side, and had been carried away—yet that could scarcely be possible, and all three insisted: "Where *is* the lorry?" The bewildered African followed their gaze, reflected, and finally grasped their thoughts.

"Lorry not fallen there. More farther—other side."

Greatly relieved, they rode the ferry across the flood. Three minutes later they found the lorry. . . .

I had been asleep. I was startled awake by a grinding noise, and in the same moment flung against a packing-case. A bag fell on my head and bounced on to Pierre, who measured his length against a petrol-drum. Hartweg was rubbing his head and his shin; Dominique was trying to extricate his leg from between a sack of rice and a folding table. We untangled ourselves and jumped out.

We were somehow balanced halfway across a little stream; the engine was reared in the air and we rested in a sort of equilibrium on the chassis members. Our truck had broken through a rotten, worm-eaten bridge and was now resting on the earthwork beneath. Nothing was broken; mercifully we had not overturned. But the platform on which we balanced was clearly about to give, and we very hastily unloaded.

Joachim hurried off to find help; we had seen road-gangs at work not far away, and very soon they were doing an effective breakdown job. Quickly and without argument they tied lianas to the lorry, and inch by inch, with tree trunks as levers, they moved us. As soon as they were confident that we would not capsize they hauled with all their strength.

The backs bent, the muscles strained and knotted; the lorry began to heave, and the planks were thrust below the tyres. Farther ahead the bridge appeared to be fairly firm. Samba decided to be brave enough to take the wheel. He slipped cautiously into gear.

The wheels spun furiously, and the motor stopped. But the bridge had not moved. The lorry seemed balanced. Everyone scattered. Samba pulled the starter

PLATE 5. The road-block: a tree, brought down by the last tornado, closes our road between Makoua and Ouesso.

PLATE 6. The forest camp of the Babenzélé Pygmies.

again, disengaged, re-engaged gently into first. The wheels began to grip, and the whole truck shuddered. "Ah!" said thirty voices tensely—and the lorry moved, passed over, stopped quietly beside the pickup.

There was nothing left to do but distribute a general thank-offering for the gang's foreman to share out among the men, and to pass round cigarettes.

There was, however, no chance now of making Ouesso before sunset. We bowled along between the walls of the forest, an inextricable confusion of wild growth, but the mud grew less.

When we halted to wait for the other truck Rouget and I got out to smoke—and there, a hundred yards before us, something had crashed through the forest like a tornado, casting aside broken branches, tearing down tree trunks, scattering leaves. A little farther on some enormous footprints explained what had happened— an elephant had passed by that morning; his traces were everywhere in the damp earth. He had blundered through the jungle's edge like an armoured division, leaving the forest wrecked until, five hundred yards farther on, he had swung off into the sheltering under-brush, and vanished.

Our two trucks were parked beside the "guest-house hut" of a little settlement buried in the forest: Moyoye. It was built of exactly the same material as everything else in the village: baked and compressed mud, lime-washed, bamboo and palm-leaf; it was main-tained by the village community and was impeccably clean. We set up our beds in two rooms opening on a large central hall, both window- and doorless—indeed, they would have been utterly useless, since there was in fact no wall. We lay, in a pleasant bedroom-dining-room-garden, against the dark background of the forest.

From the other side of the village came the sound, the approaching sound, of a song. Pierre got up from the table, looked outside and said, "Here comes the Mayor and the parish council" . . . and, sure enough, there was a gathering which must have included the entire population of the village on its way to give us a processional salutation. One of the village elders walked ahead, followed by two drummers, followed again by the women, beating gongs. The gathering built itself up into a semicircle before our floor. The headman, grizzled and dignified, came forward to shake our hands, accompanied by a splendid aide-de-camp dressed—though everyone else wore a loincloth —in a shirt and shorts.

"I am," he said, "the Corporal. I keep an eye on the roadmen. And tonight the drums are for you."

Already they had begun, pulsing out a beat for the singers. Men and women joined in the dance—they swung round, danced three steps, began again to follow each other in a steady wheeling movement. From time to time a male dancer would find himself facing a woman; he would then make a ceremonial gesture of courtesy, with the couple facing each other for several bars, until they broke away and resumed their own place in the dance.

Among them were ten dancers noticeable for their small stature: six men and four women. Their skins were of a deep ochre tint, their arms seemed unusually long, their gestures more uneven and somehow jerky. Above all, their faces were averted, held in a lowering attitude towards their breasts; always their eyes were to the ground. . . .

Could they, perhaps, be Pygmies?

I did not know, had no means of knowing, and called to Hartweg, involved with the dancers far away. When he drew near I asked him:

"You saw them? Are they really Pygmies?"

"Yes," he said, quite confidently. "I've had a close look at them. There's no doubt about it."

This was confirmed for us in a moment. "Oh, yes; they are the Babinga. There are four families of them working on the road with the local villagers."

"But since when?"

"Oh—a long time. Perhaps five months."

"Where do they live? They must have a camp— they are not all alone, surely?"

"I don't know. There may be others—but in the forest, deep in the forest."

"But where do they live? Where are their huts?"

"Near the village. They stay with the village people; that is why they are here dancing with them."

Since there was clearly no hope of any more precise explanation, we did not press the matter. Moreover these roadmen-Pygmies seemed to be wholly integrated in the local tribal life; they were not worth any great delay.

While we had been talking, the dancing had continued, but the crowd was growing thinner, and the drum-beat was clearly slackening. Suddenly, with a strange kind of military determination, the Corporal said: "Now, we go to bed. Much dancing, much tired. Tomorrow, much working on the road. Sleep well."

We rose and thanked the headman for his hospitality and drifted back to our hut. In fifteen minutes everything was quiet; a profound calm settled over the forest; nothing to be heard but a steady snoring from inside the huts. And then——

An abrupt and terrible cry awoke us all. It was repeated close at hand, seeming to come from high above our heads. Everybody listened with a sort of tense anxiety—there it was again, a kind of anguished call. A murder? An attack? There was in it some awful communication of human loss. Pierre crawled out of bed, his mosquito-net in his hand. The sound came a fourth time, but farther away. . . . The first astonishment had passed, and with it the shock of surprise; it was evident that it could not have been a cry of human fear. We went to find Samba, roused from his sleep on his seat of the lorry.

"Samba—you heard it? What is it?"

"Why, nothing——" and Samba chuckled, "——except it was monkeys. The big apes—chimpanzees, gorillas; I don't know. Certainly apes. Now they're gone, you can go back to sleep."

Now we were three weeks out of Brazzaville; that night we would be in Ouesso. Weather good, and the road good too—a highway of dense turf through bush that was no longer strange and African and impenetrable, but something like a familiar European underbrush, with the sun dancing among the shadows. Then, in front of us, Africa returned; we found a barrier across the track, where the trees had been crushed by a tornado, so that it was necessary to fetch out the axe and the machete and cut a way through the debris of broken branches. It meant several hours' delay.

At this point Dominique had a brainwave. He told Ignace and Samba to play a chorus on the lorries' horns; to press on the klaxons so that nobody for half a mile around could fail to hear it. After ten minutes of this five men appeared from the bush, each one with a hatchet in his hand. There was no need of long explanations: in half an hour the passage was cleared.

The track rose and fell between enormous trees; we moved forward through a cloud of glorious butterflies; we crossed a stream over a wooden bridge; we lunched out of tins in a village of the M'Boko people, whose job it was to maintain the roadway. And then—the sound of music, of some stringed instrument. I saw them, sitting in the doorway of a hut, with Rouget beside them. It was strange and surprising music; I had not thought to hear its like in Africa.

"What is the instrument?" I asked Rouget.

"A lute," he said.

"But it's immense! It must be about two yards long!"

"Yes," said Rouget, "it's the biggest one I have ever seen, even in the museum at home. What's more, there's another odd thing—the strings are palm-fibres, do you see, over a bridge supported on a wooden board, and underneath——"

Underneath, between the player's legs, there was an old enamelled bowl, rusted, stained, disfigured with bumps and holes.

"What is it for?"

"Just to amplify the sound."

Nobody paid any attention to our discussion; the musician played on—dreamy-eyed, plucking the strings with accomplished carelessness, his head full of some interior purpose. To his right a young man beat the end of the instrument with two long thin wands; to his left a third young man held the rhythm by shaking a condensed-milk tin filled with small stones. All three were chanting a soft recitative, always the same, always varied in small and subtle ways. We had no time to put it on record, so Rouget asked the players to catch us up at Ouesso, which was to be our base for the Pygmy-hunt.

The track became an honest road, lined with splendid palms, running between rows of huts each surrounded by small flower-gardens. We came to a warehouse with an iron roof, the post-office with its lettered sign, guest-huts, a hospital; everything made "hard"—that is to say, in brick. The track stopped on the banks of the Sangha—broad, majestically flowing. Ahead, at least five hundred yards away, rose a barrier of green—solid; a wall of growth, stained here and there by the shapes and colours of enormous flowers. This was the Forest, and in it—somewhere—the Pygmies.

Chapter III

I KNOCKED at the door of a low house surrounded
by a neat garden, with turf splashed red by clumps of
cannas; a lifeless flag hanging from a scrupulously
white-painted mast. A calm voice said: "Come in."

I pushed open the door and there was M. Mathieu,
sitting at a table littered with papers: a young and
earnest face softened by quiet blue eyes. He offered me
a seat and said:

"I was in fact waiting for you, though there's been
no message officially announcing you yet. It's surprising. I imagine the last storms must have brought
down some trees over the wire."

"We were stuck on the road ourselves ... will the
message take a long time? In any case, I have my cre-
dentials . . ." I started to look for my papers, but he
stopped me with a gesture.

"I'd been told about you by the Swedish pastor you
met at Brazzaville. A delayed telegram—what does
that matter here? Just tell me what you need from
me."

"The idea is—to get within reach of the Pygmies.
If possible, to stay with them long enough to have a
look at them, to photograph them and to record them.
Father Desfosses at Fort Rousset advised us to go as far
as Matadi and——"

55

Again he stopped me with a motion of the hand, and gave me what seemed to be a slightly ironic smile.

"Yes, I know. All right—tomorrow, in this office, you shall meet Motozélé, the headman of the Pomo-Bomassa, whose people are in touch with the Babinga. He's promised me to do what he can to guide you. I assure you that you will be in the best possible hands."

"I don't know how to thank you," I said.

"Well, wait a bit. You're not there yet. You've been long enough on the road from Brazza to have realised that between the wish and its realisation all sorts of things get in the way—nature, for example. Where are your friends?"

"Some are here, some are on the way." Then I asked, "You have not yourself been among the Pygmies?"

He made an expressive gesture at the mass of paper on his desk.

"Nevertheless, the guest-house is at your disposal. And my wife and I look forward to seeing you for dinner this evening."

Two days later, to the rhythm of a slow and stately paddle-chant, two canoes crossed the Sangha river: Jacques, Dominique and I were going with Motozélé to Gatongo, his village. From there, they said, we would be taken to the Pygmy camp. Ouesso and its houses retreated behind a waterlogged island, overgrown with liana and mangrove—everywhere we were surrounded by a gross exuberance of growth, of uninhibited vegetation: this was the beginning of the true forest that lay ahead of us. As we grounded gently against the trees foot-deep in the river a monkey leaped through the branches with shrill cries, as though it were his function to warn the secret creatures of the jungle that we were on our way.

We disembarked at Djaka on a jetty that was no more than a few planks. This was Motozélé's country. The porters loaded themselves with our gear; led us up a narrow trail. A road is marked on the map, a prolongation of the north-south track from Brazzaville to Ouesso, which is said to go to Gandikolo; the map moreover suggests that it crosses the river by a bridge. Only on the map, however. Here, from time to time, the trail broadened out into a path, but everywhere the trees and brush encroached; it was a vein through the devouring forest.

Motozélé, walking with us, spoke indifferent French, but we could understand each other. The day before, in M. Mathieu's office, our discussion had been very brief and limited to simple introductions. M. Mathieu had discussed the whole matter with him some days before. At that time Motozélé seemed a little overwhelmed by the official character of the proceedings— or possibly, as it seemed later, his shoes had merely been uncomfortably tight; for such a formal function he had felt it necessary to wear shoes, and to put on a tropical helmet, as symbol of authority. Today he wore a pair of white trousers, a shirt and a soft hat. He was certainly no more than thirty-five years old. In our scraps of conversation I gathered how he had become chief of the Pomo.

"My father died last year," he said; "he was chief of the Pomo and the Bomassa. All the villages came for the burying; everyone met at Gatongo." He paused for a moment, and took off his shoes. "In this country, need *espadrilles*," he said, looking approvingly at my

57

feet. He knotted his laces, threw his shoes over his shoulder and went on, "Well, when the people got there they had an election. They chose me; and here I am, chief of the Pomo-Bomassa. The Administration agreed, of course."

"How many villages do you control?"

He thought for a minute, and then said, with pride, "Twenty-one. But Djaka isn't really a village; it is only two houses—and Gatongo, my village, is really two villages, Gatongo I and Gatongo II. The old governor changed it."

I noticed that the trail now ran between bushes with dense, small leaves and red berries—undoubtedly coffee, but choked with weeds, the bushes suffocated by creepers and tendrils. They looked doomed. Motozélé explained that this had once been a prosperous plantation, established by the governor-before-last—the business had lapsed, gone to seed. That was the reason for the displacing of the Gatongo villagers.

After three hours' walk we came on a cluster of three or four huts among the trees: Gatongo I. We were invited to rest awhile in one of the huts by its proprietor— he was a smith, making and selling spearheads and axes to the neighbouring hunters. He did well, it seemed, for there was little competition in the forest. Before we left he made a point of telling us, with a slightly lofty air, that he was a Muslim. It seemed surprising, for apart from the trading Hausa tribesmen there are few Mohammedans in the forest. Motozélé confirmed this; he had been converted to Islam during a visit to the North, and now he was headman of the twin Gatongos.

Sometime that afternoon we came to Gatongo II— some twenty huts or so, which I shall call simply

Gatongo from now on. Out to meet us came Alexandre Djambabo—young, dressed in khaki shirt and shorts, the clerk of Motozélé. With him was Logoué, the local "constable", who wore a loincloth of vivid colours, his mobile face flickering in turn with good humour and slyness. The porters carried our gear to the guest-hut at the end of the village. Joachim and Leonard—a young Baya we had hired in Ouesso as interpreter—prepared a quick meal, for we had more visiting to do with Motozélé.

We took the same trail we had used in the morning. Alexandre told us that it continued as far as Bomassa and Nola in Oubangui-Chari, where it turned into a regular road. If the section between Ouesso and Nola could only be put in order there would be a reliable driving link between this part of the forest and the Middle Congo. At the moment there was nothing—except the aeroplane, and the river-boats.

Outside the village the track ran between plantations. Then, a few yards farther, was the half-hidden footpath that led to the Pygmies' base camp. As we followed Motozélé he told us that there were in fact no Pygmies there—tomorrow we could go into the forest and seek them out, but today. . . . There, in a clearing among the great trunks, were the huts, some of them a yard high and two yards across at floor-level, others a little bigger. Some had little annexes: tiny hut-ments even smaller.

"For the *moana*, the children," explained Logoué; but he was anxious to hurry on, we had some miles to go yet. At Gandikolo the trail dipped towards the Sangha river. Here we loaded our heavy equipment on to a boat to save the porters' backs. Life moved gently among the huts: a few women sat at their doors preparing the manioc flour, suckling a baby; an old woman played drowsily with the children. Motozélé enquired where Akili, the village chief was, but he was away in his canoe; we would see him that evening on our return.

Half a mile farther on two straw-huts by the trail announced a tiny hamlet that had been christened by its founder: "Lookout". He was an old soldier of the first World War—and there he sat, in an ancient military hat, framed in the doorway of his hut. He had a grizzled beard and was of great dignity. I asked him why he had called his home "Lookout", and the answer was immediate, in a loud and ringing voice.

"Lookout? Why—Look out for the wizards, to see they do not come near *me*."

At Kombo-Kombo we were in the Baya country. These people came from the Nola district some sixty miles north; they tapped rubber in the forest. All the men were away; they would not return for three weeks, until the September market at Ouesso. The headman, Békondo, welcomed us with flattering eagerness; it seemed no white man had passed his way for many months. I noticed two heaps of large seeds, or grains; I took them to be peanuts—until Dominique and I examined some in our hands: they were dried caterpillars. Motozélé laughed at our surprise. He took one and handed it to Jacques.

"You can eat it."

They had no odour whatever. We nibbled them rather dubiously—the skin split between the teeth, and the taste of slightly off-colour nut was not offensive. Békondo disappeared into his hut and came out with a calabash of palm-wine. After this curious refreshment we moved on, Békondo with us, towards another Baya camp called Mogo, where the headman offered us eggs, and tailed on to the escort. We were a sizeable party by the time we reached N'Dalo, the Yassoua village.

The chief of this place, Nganda, wanted us to hear his three-piece xylophone orchestra, which was noted in the neighbourhood. The best musicians were not able to perform, as they were tapping rubber in the forest; we had to have the substitute performers—two old men and a child. The three instruments were identical except for a variation in the size. They consisted of a scale of wooden blades in a frame with calabashes arranged vertically below them as resonators. The musicians tapped the wooden scales with sticks, attacking the same melodic phrase. After a while I detected differences in the seemingly identical xylophones—the biggest had eleven notes, with a hollower and slightly deeper pitch; the smallest had eight, in a treble pitch; the middle instrument had nine notes, pitched somewhere between the two. The two old men and the child changed their tune; I heard it clinking in my ears as we took to the road again.

We walked through the darkness, following the white shirt that marked Motozélé. One by one the village headmen dropped away. At Gandikolo, Akili awaited us beside a fire built in the open; he made us welcome with the gift of a cockerel. With his white hair, his regular features and his gentle eyes, he had an expression curiously sweet, yet detached and reflective. After his formal welcome he did not speak again, but remained thoughtful and silent; a strange remote man who looked as though he should talk to no one but the spirits of the dead. When we left him he took our hands and held them long between his own, as though he wished to communicate to each of us some secret message, intended for us alone. He was a Biblical figure, a patriarch.

We covered the last mile like automatons, for we had walked all day. Motozélé gave us a bottle of palm-oil, and we stretched ourselves out in genuine fatigue. Outside, the humidity of the night condensed into heavy drops of water; they fell like erratic rain on the palm roof over us.

It was a dismal dawn, under a sky charged with clouds so thick and black that the forest ahead of us looked like the wall of a fortress, a dense barrier without, it seemed, the slightest opening or loophole. We dressed hurriedly, and the porters approached, introducing themselves: N'Koundé, Dayama, Yaboto, Dapané. We packed our beds on to the porters' baskets: a simple back-harness capable of supporting a big load.

Joachim poured us tea, and the scalding stuff on my lips managed finally to rouse me. Motozélé arrived with Alexandre Djambabo, who was solicitous about the comfort of our night's rest. We reassured him; he in his turn reassured us—he had caused us a little concern the previous night with an insect that had made its way deep into his ear. The operation of removing it had taken an hour. Today, he was all smiles.

The sun was up; a toucan on a nearby branch saluted it with a shrill scream. Motozélé gave the order to march. Then the porter Dayama stepped forward—he spoke for his friends, he said, and Alexandre explained: they were willing to carry for us, and they would follow us along the track, but . . . they would not enter the forest. They would not risk having to cross the *poto-poto*, the boglands.

I handed over the job of persuading them to Motozélé. He took Alexandre aside and conferred for a moment, then called the porters over. For a while there was the murmur of his voice, phrases emphasised with movements of the head, the echo of approval from his clerk. By the time his harangue was over the porters were ready.

At seven o'clock our little column began to move along the track between the plantations of manioc and corn, heavily shadowed by the undergrowth. We were in the forest, forced into a close Indian file behind the leader, who cleared the path with a machete, with Motozélé and Alexandre behind him. I followed Alexandre; Jacques and Dominique, Leonard and Joachim followed me. We did not speak, it needed too much concentration to place our feet in the footsteps of the man ahead, to fend aside the dead branches, the huge leaves, to avoid the twisted roots. Very soon, it seemed, one acquired the reflexes of a track runner. While my limbs went through their routine of avoiding, warding off, plodding on, my thoughts wandered away. The expedition had at last got us here, into the final forest; each step brought us nearer to the Pygmies. Motozélé had promised to produce them before the end of the day. Alexandre, more prudent, warned us that the Babinga would be warned of our coming, and would retreat deeper into the woods before our advance.

We came into a clearing among the great trees, and there—I had seen them at the Pygmies' base camp near Gatongo—were the tiny huts, scattered in an attractive disorder round a rough circle. The central space, doubtless reserved for dances and meetings, was overgrown by thick vegetation. A patch of burned earth marked some vanished home. The other huts were falling to bits; they were made on a foundation of rods thrust into the earth, bent and interlaced in a shape more or less hemispherical and covered with large leaves, already dry and crumbling.

While the porters caught us up we examined the camp abandoned by the Babinga. The name means "hunters"; the word does not designate a tribe; it is simply a generic term given to the Pygmies by the local Africans. We waited no longer but took to the track again, with a stimulated eagerness to see the little owners of these huts.

The enormous cushion of cloud that overhung the roof of the forest rose gradually. The sun climbed through the branches, and very soon it began to dry the dew-soaked underbrush. Walking became more pleasant—until, suddenly, we found ourselves plunging through a floor that had become a sponge. Not a bird sang, not an animal stirred; there was no sound but the swish of the leaves as we passed among them, wordlessly. How much longer before we found the Pygmy camp? I was resigned already to several days' march in this forest—competing with the vegetable labyrinth, the mind playing round and round with the images of what had already been: the organisation, the administration, the waiting in anterooms, the official arguments, corridors, stairs, waiting-rooms, double doors, telephones, offices, letters, good wishes, regrets . . . and now, today, it had all culminated in this: the silent steps of the man ahead in the depths of the virgin forest.

PLATE 7. A Pygmy woman, one of the Babinga Bangombé.

PLATE 8. Bakembé, a member of the Babenzélé tribe.

Chapter IV

The Trail through the Bog – Pygmies at Last – Night among the Babenzélé – The Rubber Men.

MOTOZÉLÉ stopped abruptly. The marshy track had become a bog, saturated with the early rains. We decided to wait for the porters to catch us up so that we could cross together, hoping that it would be neither too wide nor too deep.

Dayama arrived ahead, with three companions, followed a few minutes later by Yaboto and Dapané. They were old comrades of the track; they came from the same villages. We sat on a fallen tree and passed round a packet of cigarettes while we waited for the others. Motozélé wanted to know if France were indeed, as everyone seemed to say, a land of perpetual cold and mud. Dominique reached into his pocket for a photograph of a sunlit snow scene—the Africans studied it with curiosity and a complete lack of comprehension. We tried to explain, but snow meant nothing to them.

After a brief rest we faced the *poto-poto* again. It seemed to cross the forest for several miles; the dense black liquid climbed first to our shins, then to our knees, a soupy mess that smelt putrid and probably was. Several times our sandals were sucked off; there was then the awkward business of hanging by one hand to any support and groping in the noisome muck; and all the while the lianas and branches threatened to trip one into the mud. I was anxious about my camera gear around my neck. The porters were admirable, stepping with equilibrium under a head-load of forty pounds.

After half an hour of this the bog began to clarify, and as a gentle current propelled the mud towards the tall walls of the forest another danger arose, that of finding no foothold at all. Motozélé, however, knew a secret track laid across the marsh by the Africans and Pygmies, a sort of submerged bridge of logs that had somehow to be identified below the surface by the groping feet. Several times I missed my step and had to grab for Alexandre's staff. This underwater causeway was the only thing that prevented us from having to wade chin-deep. It lasted for some three hundred yards, and then the ground solidified beneath our feet. We climbed up a little slope and found a clear stream where we could wash away some of the filth of the bog while the sun filtered through from above with a sort of submarine light and glittered on the tepid water.

Alexandre, drying his hands on his shirt-tails, came up to me and said confidentially:

"Tell me, M. Noël—why are you and your friends trying to find the Babinga?"

His interest pleased me and embarrassed me too—how was I to explain to him the impulse that had caused us all these months of difficulties and exasperations? It was, after all, only the discovery of a new sort of world.

"The Pygmies hide themselves in the forest, we know that, but we want to meet them, and live among them. We've got to find them."

66

It was an unconvincing argument. To Alexandre, what mattered was to investigate the "white man's way"; he was a practical man—from the "white man's way" he could learn things to his advantage. He hesitated, then said, almost indignantly:

"But, M. Noël—why the Babinga? They are dirty. They are ugly, and they smell bad."

It was even harder to explain to him that such a summary picture tended to excite my curiosity even more.

We set off again through an open undergrowth among the enormous trunks of the cotton-trees, tall columns thirty, fifty, even sixty yards high above our heads, seemingly sleek and glossy to the summit, groping hugely for the light. This was the great primeval forest. Somewhere high above us the sun burned, but here there was almost a breeze. It felt good. We walked along at a brisk pace.

Now, according to the information Motozélé had obtained from a local monkey-hunter, the camp of the Babinga should not be far away.

And two hours later, there it was. Through the brush came the sound of voices, of axe-blows, the cries of children, and the Pygmies at last were only a matter of yards ahead. Motozélé stopped us. It was imperative that he go ahead and warn them of our coming, for they had never before seen white men, and our faces, our clothes, our movements would certainly alarm them.

It was a moment of some importance. We could do no more than wait for the result of Motozélé's introduction. Would he be able to persuade them of our peaceful intentions? If the Pygmies were nervous, so indeed were we. Any clumsiness on our part, any abrupt movement or too emphatic words would send them scampering away deeper and deeper into the forest, far into the marshlands of the Epéna. It was a long quarter of an hour waiting for Motozélé.

Alexandre made a sign for me to approach. I went forward a few paces, and there was the camp—the clearing, the huts, an open space, with the men sitting around in a half-circle. As far as I could see, the women had taken refuge in the shadow of the huts, and with them the children. In complete silence every gaze was turned on us. Motozélé, standing upright, presented us to the camp's chief, whose name was Mougounzi, and who stood up with a quick movement. I was struck at first sight by the vivacity and intelligence of his expression. He was dressed in one piece of cloth, his skin a deep ochre, his head completely shaven except for a small tuft above the brow. He wore a moustache, but was unbearded. It seemed to me that he was no more than four feet tall, but his body was well-made and strong.

One by one we shook him by the hand, and sat down on little wooden stools set out for us. Mougounzi remained surrounded by a group of men apparently older than himself, who gave the appearance of constituting a sort of council.

To open the meeting diplomatically, I offered them a bag of salt. At once their eyes gleamed: a good omen. Alexandre interpreted their words.

"This is the first time your people have come to see us. We were afraid."

We too, I said to myself, we were afraid, we never thought we would get this far.

"Motozélé has explained why you have come. You are very welcome to stay in our camp."

It seemed very like success. We thanked them.

Jacques asked if the invitation included him. He was told it did. He went on: "Noël and Dominique will go and find the rest of our party with our equipment," and the reply again was immediate. "You may all come. You are our friends."

I made haste to offer tobacco all round, and sugar for the children. I questioned Alexandre about our hosts' intentions concerning their next camp. Jacques wanted to film them crossing the lake to establish their base camp for the harvest season. This enquiry started a lively discussion between Mougounzi and the Elders, who began to look unpleasantly at us and talk vigorously in their own language. Another round of tobacco did not noticeably conciliate them. Alexandre explained to me that the Pygmies had already been encamped there for two weeks; it was necessary for them to move on to new hunting-grounds, and that although Mougounzi had no objection to remaining, the Elders were dead against it; they insisted on leaving tomorrow. The move had been prepared, they had no intention of changing their arrangements. It did not seem a good idea to argue.

After another distribution of tobacco the Pygmies, of their own accord, began to clear a corner of the forest for our camp, at some little distance from their own. This suggested, as did this first exchange of opinions, that in spite of their hospitality the Pygmies remained jealous of their independence. As far as hunting was concerned, which is their only form of livelihood, there was no question of changing their customs.

They quickly erected a large pent-roof of leaves, and we put up our beds and mosquito-nets. While I was writting up my diary a delegation approached us, and Alexandre introduced me to an old man—Télé, father

69

of Mougounzi—whose grizzled beard I had noticed earlier. The committee sat in the usual semicircle and Télé solemnly repeated:

"We are your friends. We will tell you the secrets of our hearts."

"We are very grateful. We are your friends. Later, when we return to our own people, we shall tell them how the Babenzélé received us, and how they live in their forest."

They approved this, but there still remained a question of economics.

"You come to us with salt and tobacco. You also have shirts and trousers. We have nothing. We want salt with which to eat our meat, tobacco to put in the pipe, and cigarettes, we want *machetes* to cut our paths through the wood, and loincloths."

"Tell them we shall provide all these things."

They went away. It was impossible to know if they were pleased or not; they knew how to keep an impassive expression in which courtesy mingled with great dignity.

It was five o'clock, and dusk spread among the trees. The camp had resumed its normal activities as though we had not been there. The women began to prepare the evening meal.

Alexandre stayed near us. Jacques, preoccupied by his filming, already wanted to know where the Babenzélé hunted elephant and gorilla. The elephant, which has moved eastwards, is rather rare in this district, they said, and as for the gorilla, he was hunted only occasionally. When they could, they hunted the antelope. While we talked, a Pygmy brought us a *boloko*—a tiny gazelle no bigger than a kid—laid it at the foot of a bed and departed silently.

Was this present, offered without remark, a delicate reply to our gifts to them, a mark of courtesy? As I lay there in the growing darkness I recalled a phrase I once read in an ethnological paper: "Gifts are an exchange of graces." Here it took on complete significance.

The little *boloko* provided our dinner. We had hardly finished when Motozélé and Mougounzi came for us. The entire camp was now gathered round the fire, the men in front, the women behind, with the babies in their arms and the toddlers between their knees. They began to sing.

The men and the women sang together, and even the children raised their voices with all their heart. We stared at them, deeply impressed, there was something gripping about the religious intensity of the song.

So it went on, under the stars, a chorus always renewing itself, losing itself in the night, like hymns in an endless cathedral.

Before first light the camp was again awake. It was five o'clock. Alexandre and Motozélé, who had spent the night under a shelter of leaves, told us that the Pygmies were astir earlier than usual to prepare for the camp's departure. At once everyone seemed on the move, busied with his or her special task. While the men gathered up the bundles of sticks and the hanks of fibres from which they make their nets, the women collected the cooking vessels, the earthen pots and the wooden mortars. Their very few precious possessions— like the salt—were carefully parcelled up in the big leaves from the hut roofs.

I saw two Pygmies scratching a hole in the ground, under the direction of Mougounzi. They lined it with leaves, and emptied into it the contents of an earthen vessel: a clear liquid in which floated bits of bark. I asked Alexandre what they were doing.

"They're preparing rubber for Motozélé."

Without delay they poured into this decoction a milky-white liquid, the rubber-sap they had gathered the previous days; as it fell into the liquid it coagulated instantly into thin strips of a white pasty substance, faintly translucent: raw rubber.

At last the community was ready to break camp. The women disappeared under vast loads, bent double; they supported the burden by a thong passed round the forehead, their load covering them from their head to the back of their knees. The babies were suspended in a sort of sling of fibre or hide, so that when they cried they could easily be put to the breast. The men bore on their shoulders the big hunting-nets, which weighed up to thirty pounds, and in their hands they held either a spear or an axe. The girls, too, carried loads, though lesser ones than their mothers, and the boys carried sometimes the end of a net or a hank of fibre, and sometimes a stick of wood that acted as a very slow-burning torch, soon to be used to light the new fire. Mougounzi bore a drum. We followed him, and one by one the caravan moved off into the under-brush.

We walked through the forest all the morning, along an entirely different track from that of the day before. There was no hesitation; the Pygmies marked their course by a slowly-rotting tree trunk, by a liana covered with some curious excrescence, or by a staff planted in the ground. It was clear that the forest is home to the Babinga; much more so than to the other Africans. Rapidly, silently, confidently, they slipped through the labyrinth. I was curious to know how they would manage the crossing of the bog, and was hardly surprised when, on reaching the stream, there was a tree firmly laid across it. This route must have been known only to them. On the other side of the stream the ground was firm to the feet; the bog itself must have lain downstream. There were more tree-trunk bridges ahead, and Jacques was annoyed at having no camera, so deft and sure were the movements of these heavily-burdened people, like tight-rope walkers. If by chance any of them found themselves in difficulty there was always a comrade's arm to help, especially if it were a mother carrying a sleeping baby.

Motozélé had warned us that there would be about five hours of this journey. We must now be very near to the site of the new Pygmy camp. And, indeed, just ahead came the sound of guttural voices and quick laughter, and there in a narrow clearing the advance party had already begun to install the settlement. Some cleared the brush, others hurried off to get poles, and the women gathered the big phrynium leaves with which they would roof the huts. In a few hours enough had been done for the first night; the refinements of construction would be left for next day.

We sat on our luggage and shared out the remains of yesterday's meal, some rice and what was left of the gazelle. We decided to set up our quarters where we could have an unimpeded view of the life of the Pygmies. As we ate, every mouthful was punctuated by slaps on the arms and legs, for there was an almost unsupportable company of insects—mosquitoes, and a tiny sort of fly which was nearly invisible but which had an intolerable sting.

"Well—I hope you have a good night, in spite of this."

73

"Don't worry. If this carries on, Leonard will know how to get rid of them."

Leonard, who had been following this, said eagerly, "Oh, yes, sir."

"At least," said Jacques, "I can shelter in the mosquito-net."

"The net? These wretched little flies will easily get through."

"The thing to do," said Dominique, "is to put several nets over each other. We shall leave you ours."

For, in fact, we had brought too few provisions for us all, and it was agreed that only one of us could stay with the Pygmies; that Jacques should remain with Leonard. He would spend the time of waiting in working out his script for filming the Babinga. He would not have to be long alone; it was now Saturday, and by Monday Trotty and Dominique would return with cameras and film. To simplify their own movements they were going to leave most of their bedding.

Jacques was well contented with his position, alone with the Pygmies in the forest, and we would willingly have changed places with him.

"A little dose of the simple life," he said, laughing, "that's what one needs to make one value one's comforts later." And I took a letter he had hurriedly scribbled for his wife.

Four hours later we were well on our way down the track to Gatongo and Gandikolo. We had not realised how nearly the Pygmies had approached this in yesterday's march. It would certainly facilitate our return with the equipment.

Here we said good-bye to Alexandre and Motozélé. It was very hard to thank them sufficiently for their help, their good-nature and for the fact that through

74

them alone we had made our contact with the Pygmies.

At Gandikolo, Akili was waiting with his grandson Zabou, a little fellow of four. Two canoes were ready; the boatmen knew the river and its currents. Joachim was returning with us, full of his experience; when he next saw his village and Brazzaville he would have a grand time telling of his adventures in the forest. Now, sitting in the well of the canoe, he amused himself— and the boatmen and porters—by playing with a team of huge caterpillars he had gathered in the woods and kept carefully in a parcel of leaves. They were about five inches long, of an orange colour, their skins tight as a sausage; they propelled themselves along, agitating short active antennae topped by a bright point of eye. Joachim attached each by the tail to a thin blade of grass, and to amuse him the porters pretended to bet on the individual caterpillar's speed and strength.

As the night fell the caterpillars went back into Joachim's pocket. We went ashore at Ouesso, at a little wooden jetty. Behind it were the shapes of Didier and Trotty. Dominique hailed them.

"Hallo, there!"

"Greetings!"

"Where's Jacques?"

"He's waiting with the Pygmies. The real Pygmies!"

"Are they far away?"

"We left them only this afternoon. The camp is superb. Motozélé is a wonder. We'll tell you all about it. . . ."

Chapter V

The Lonely Troubadour — Visit to the Swedes — Among the Sandbanks — Village Medicine — Back among the Pygmies — The Champion Drummers.

TROTTY and Dominique left to join Jacques in a Greek trader's pinnace that would carry them as far as Gandikolo. They took ten porters, the Eyemo and the Arriflex cameras, six tins of film and a large tent to serve as a laboratory.

We were to wait where we were for the boat that would carry our major stores: the flour, rice, concentrated milk, the highly important bottles of brandy and the recording gear. Clearly we should not be able to leave Ouesso before Wednesday, 28th August. M. Mathieu, to whom I had reported our reconnaissance with the Pygmies, was to lend us the Government pinnace, but it was under repair and would not be available for forty-eight hours.

While we had been away Didier and Rouget had been classifying and packing the recordings we had made since leaving Brazzaville. Hartweg, in the hospital, continued his blood-group studies. Pierre was making his sketches and preparing his canvases.

That afternoon we went to bathe in the Sangha. At the water's edge a man was sitting on a big stone. In his left hand he held a little bow, the sort of little bow a child makes, a slender stick and a thin fibre; he was playing this thing somehow in the manner of a Jew's-

76

harp. The string passed between his lips while with his right hand he tapped it gently with a light bamboo; he was humming a sombre chant, murmuring some strange plaint to the empty river. As I watched this curious reverie Rouget came up and sat beside us.

"It's a musical bow," he explained, "one of the most primitive stringed instruments in the world. We recorded it on Friday while you were in the forest. We were working with a zither player we met on the road when this man came up and volunteered."

"But why does he keep his mouth open?"

"It acts as a sort of sounding-board. As he opens or closes it more or less he gets different tones. You see how he touches the string with the little stick, and gets another harmonic."

Moving quietly away, so as not to disturb this lonely troubadour, Rouget told me what he had heard from the doctor.

"That man—he's a M'Boko—is an old sleeping-sickness case. He's been cured, but his mind was affected. You saw his empty look and his perpetual smile. He spent such a long time in the hospital that he still haunts the place, playing his little tunes among the patients."

The doctor of Ouesso was from Martinique, a man of great courtesy and charm, with racial origins somewhat approaching those of the Africans. When he was not on duty he spent his time touring the villages of the subdivision; we had little time to chat with him, for he was often away.

Everyone was at pains to be friendly and helpful. We were the guests of M. Thébault, agent of the Compagnie Française du Haut et Bas Congo, who was to deliver our provisions—but the river-boat *Balin*, it seemed, was aground on a sandbank; the rains were

77

late and the Sangha was low; we could not expect the boat for a week. The Company's engineer also had us round for a Pernod, and talked to us in a rich Parisian accent of the place Pigalle and the foire du Trône; he had not seen France for nine years. A flock of little mulatto imps ran around underfoot. He was happy here with his children and the "housekeeper", a quiet, grave and attractive young woman.

Hartweg and Rouget went to see the Swedish pastor —he was not in, but his wife and daughter received them. As they sat in comfortable chairs, behind calico curtains, the conversation was not exactly an animated one; the good ladies knew only three words of French, 'It is hot", which they murmured in turn at intervals, demonstrating the accuracy of this observation with profound sighs. Rouget and Hartweg, utterly ignorant of any Scandinavian phrases, responded to this with a succession of understanding smiles. The visit lasted an hour and a half, after which the ladies rose and thanked them for their call.

That afternoon we paid another call, on the two red-bearded Alsatian Fathers. In the Presbytery dining-room, before a statue of Our Lady of Lourdes, they offered us a pleasant orange-wine of their own manufacture. After the usual preambles of the district—the weather, and the lateness of the mail—Hartweg asked them if they had ever come across the Pygmies.

"The Pygmies? Oh dear, no. To see them you have to go into the forest. Here we have enough to do—we are building a new church, out of bricks, too."

The Father showed us the plans: a little suburban church with a pointed belfry.

"We are waiting for the statues. They come from Paris. It takes a long time."

78

"But why not have them made locally?" I asked the Father. "These village craftsmen can do some lovely work."

"No use at all. I assure you, these people are good for nothing."

We glanced at each other, refraining from argument, and made our excuses to go. Such a categorical judgement, from the mouth of a missionary, alarmed me; I had not thought to come up against such prejudice at Ouesso. I felt suddenly anxious to be with Akili, Motozélé, and Mougounzi again.

It took all our efforts to load the pinnace with our gear. The previous evening we had separated the stuff we would not take with us, such as the exposed film and the records already made.

With the rest of it, we set off upstream. The helmsman knew the currents well; we had time and leisure to watch the wooded banks on either side. Suddenly Pierre, who carried his carbine on his knees, pulled it to his shoulder and fired. "A crocodile!" He had been sunning himself on a bank; I glimpsed him just before he dived. "You saw how small he was, with that long, narrow muzzle," exclaimed Hartweg. "He reminded me of the gaviales in India."

Quite abruptly the pinnace ran aground. The helmsman remained impassive, but he was clearly shocked. He could be excused easily enough; the channels were always shifting among the sandbanks, especially here, where we were, at the junction of the N'Goko, full of complicated islets. The assistant-helmsman climbed into the water and discovered we were in an extensive system of shallows. We drifted off, unable for a moment or two to do anything but allow the stream to take us into deeper water. Starting the engine we tried again. To the right we ran at once into sunken branches. We turned to the other side; there it became necessary to breast a serious current between the sandbanks and the river's edge, so near that the overhanging trees scraped us—luckily none of them were strong enough to stop us; they bent and broke, and we passed on.

Once past the sandbanks the man at the tiller relaxed again, and in the middle of the afternoon, under the palms, we landed at Gandikolo. The village, hidden behind the trees, was marked by the strings of canoes by the shore. A child who saw us climb out alerted the village, and the whole population came running—the whole population, that is, without the men. Nevertheless, even among the women and children there was competition as to who should carry the heaviest boxes and the most unwieldy crates. We had to check this enthusiasm for the sake of some of the more delicate equipment. Before we could at last get our bathe in the river we had to do the climb up to the travellers' hut many times. With the boxes and bags stowed inside the bamboo walls, the place became a goods-yard. We put up our own hammocks and beds in the open; we would sleep beneath the stars—praying for no rain.

Before leaving for the Babenzélé camp Didier had taken the recording gear to Gatongo. There was no need to record the Pygmies in the heart of the forest, since in any case they would soon have to return to their base. Meanwhile he took charge of a camera, to help Jacques. Hartweg, Nief, Rouget and Lods were here, but there could be no question of our descending on the Pygmies all together, especially in the early days. We wanted to run no risk of scaring them off by a mass arrival; we

PLATE 9. Pygmy children of the Babenzélé tribe.

PLATE 10. (*above*) The three-piece xylophone orchestra of the Yassoua. (*below*) Instruments borrowed by the Pygmies from the Pomo Africans: a wickerwork rattle and an iron bell.

would have enough trouble, as it was, familiarising them with the camera itself.

I had warned Alexandre of our return and asked him to send us porters. The messenger brought me a reply, in a huge handwriting, signed: "The Writer", which said: "Ha, Monsieur Noël, the porters are changing behind you, wait for us tomorrow morning." At the same time there was a note from Trotty: "We have reached the Babinga camp. The porters were wonderful and I advise you to use them again." If I understood rightly, this meant that the porters who had gone on with Trotty and Dominique had returned to Ouesso, and Motozélé was trying to recall them. We should have to be patient for a day.

However, quite early in the morning Alexandre arrived to tell us that the porters had been rounded up and that we should be able to join Jacques and the others by that evening.

The morning passed rapidly. Hartweg—who had studied medicine for some years before specialising in anthropology—was busy practising on the villagers. As soon as they saw him distributing his medicines everyone discovered himself the victim of some incurable malady that needed immediate attention. For all that, there were several very genuine cases: a woman with a bad abscess on the thigh, a baby with horribly running eyes, swarming with flies. There was also a good market for laxatives, for headache-powders, ointment for sores and ulcers.

During this time Rouget was making an investigation into the local pottery, with Didier taking the pictures. I went with them, and told Rouget that I had seen almost identical pottery in the Babinga camp. Without doubt, the Africans provided the Pygmies with their pots. The women who made the stuff sought their material, a grey clay, from the river bank, and we spent some time watching one old woman in her process of manufacture. First she took several lengths of clay, long smooth sausages, and modelled her pot by laying them one above the other, smoothing the work occasionally with a wooden spatula. The shape of the vessel was roughly spherical, with an orifice finished with a slightly turned-back ridge. Beside the potter a couple of completed pots stood on a lattice of bamboo. On either side of the belly of the pots were two short, robust handles, with a fluted decoration. Easily dried in the sun, the pots are baked in the simplest imaginable way: they are covered in a pile of shavings and brushwood which is set on fire. It not infrequently happens that this, the last part of the operation, reduces them to fragments.

Under the palms not far from our hammocks a man was digging out a canoe from the solid tree. The first part of this job is done by burning away the central cavity in the trunk. A young woman and her little girl sat in front of their hut grinding manioc, dried in the sun, into the fine white flour from which they would make their pancakes.

We were expecting ten porters; by afternoon only four had showed up. Our comrades ahead were certainly going to wonder what had happened to us.

As we were congratulating the cook, who had contrived to make some excellent bread in a hole in the ground, Akili came up to invite us to watch the dance. We went, but in spite of the energy of the drummers and the civilities of Akili it was not a particularly amusing spectacle, since most of the usual performers were not there. The only noticeable dancer was the old lady who had been making the pots. Armed with a cane, she whirled around with such speed that at any moment we expected to see her spin into the middle of the spectators. As she neared us she broke into an excess of bows and reverences, threatened us with her rod, shouted imprecations and returned to her dizzy dancing, shouting stridently. This old shrew interested and irritated me at the same time. It seemed that our presence was at least in some way responsible for this demonstration, and we had decided to retire, when there was a sudden upsurge of drumming and more dancers appeared. And this time they were Pygmies.

We were astonished to see the Babinga in this N'Goundi village, but there it was, they were there. Rouget indicated the little people to an African standing beside him; the Pygmies were seized by a curious vibration from head to foot, dancing with a jerky movement, extraordinarily rapid.

"Those are Babinga? Where do they come from?"

"They are Babinga Bangombé, they come from the Cameroons, from the far side of the river. But their huts are behind the village."

This man, Amenga (who was henceforth to be a faithful interpreter for Rouget), thus revealed to us the existence of another tribe of Pygmies existing only a few hundred yards from Gandikolo.

For three hours we had been marching through the forest. We hoped to get in touch with our filming friends before nightfall. We were accompanied by four porters and Bernard, the young man who had replaced Joachim, whom we had left lying ill in the hospital at Ouesso. They were very heavily laden, and to relieve them we had each of us taken one burden over and above our personal affairs. Didier carried the tool box; he was far-sighted enough not to want to be separated from this, as possibly a camera might have to be repaired and the soldering-lamp was in any case essential for sealing the tins of exposed film. For my part, I carried a bag with ten tins of condensed milk.

After an hour or more I began to worry. Dapané assured me we were doing well; I wanted to believe him, and in the absence of any particularly recognisable trail there was nothing for it but to trust him. I shifted my bag to the other shoulder—the boots inside it hurt my back; Didier bore his load like an African, on the head. So we pushed on along the invisible track.

Twenty minutes later I lifted my eyes to see, three yards over the guide's shoulder, a splash of khaki colour: a tent appeared among the branchy shadows— and so, at last, there we were. We let ourselves collapse on a seat of logs around a table. Jacques, Trotty and Dominique raised their heads.

"Well," they said, "and about time too. Luckily Motozélé said you'd arrived at Gandikolo. We've been waiting."

Jacques pulled out of his pocket a letter in a handwriting that I recognised as Alexandre's, although it was signed "Motozélé".

"My good friends Jacques, Séchan and Dominique," I read. "I am happy to get news from Monsieur Alexandre, who has told me about you. What happened? It cannot be the oil which you went to buy in my village. There was a mistake. I send you a bottle of palm-oil by the hand of Commanda for which there shall be no charge. Here are five francs from the hand of Commanda, my brother's replacement. You are come here to tell me everything. Ha! The friends are arrived yesterday and they are six white men whose name I do not know, except for Noël. Alexandre is gone to Gandikolo to deliver the letter of Séchan. I have nothing to say. Alexandre wishes you good-day. Your Bokeli— (the word was erased, then translated)—your friend, Motozélé."

"You see you are on excellent terms with the authorities. Motozélé is a good-hearted man."

I handed the letter to André and turned to Jacques.

"Well—this dose of the simple life, how was it?"

"Upon my word, it has passed very well. I've had company every day. Koukilemba, Motozélé's brother, came and stayed until the headman arrived with baskets of manioc, which I shared round among the Pygmies. After Trotty and Dominique arrived, Alexandre and Koukilemba showed up again and helped us to put up the tent and this splendid dining-room."

"What about the flies?"

"It was absolutely intolerable for the first two days. They were everywhere—in the milk and in the jam, and the little brutes have a sort of sharp taste which is far from pleasant. Luckily they go away at night. But for the last two days it has seemed as though there weren't so many. A question of getting used to them."

André put in: "That's all very well. What about the test photography?"

Trotty showed some developed strips. The previous day they had filmed a little gazelle, a small boy playing by a hut, and several Pygmy activities, all without the Pygmies knowing. André examined the film.

"It's good. The light seems enough."

"Yes. From ten in the morning till four in the afternoon, though you have to chase the patches of sun

85

when there are any. With two cameras we'll get along faster."

"And your beds—where have you put them?"

"The Pygmies put up a big pent-roof of leaves—fairly solid, though it was an absolute shower-bath to begin with. Now it's all right. Best of all, though, it's only a few yards from the Babinga huts; when you don't want to alarm the people it makes a superb observatory."

"And how are you getting on with the Pygmies?"

"Excellently. Every day they bring us meat; so much of it in fact that, when we've chosen as much as we need, Leonard takes them back a *boloko* or a *n'gandi*."

"A what?"

"A *n'gandi*. It's an antelope about as big as a new-born calf, with a splendid ruddy hide and a brown stripe on the back. You needn't be afraid we shall be short of meat. What about the other stuff? The boat came, I suppose? Did you bring the provisions?"

"No, the *Balin* didn't come, it was stuck on a sand-bank. We've brought rice and a little oil, condensed milk, and a couple of loaves of home-baked bread, which is a bit of a success."

While we talked we had arranged the provisions, and Leonard and Pascal (who had accompanied the film men) prepared the meal round the fire. The porters had put their manioc cakes on to cook.

I was eager to meet the Pygmies again. I went back with Jacques to our dormitory, a hundred yards from the dining place. Four beds were lined up under the leafy roof; there was a space left for a fifth. In the dusk, with their mosquito-nets already set, they looked like motionless boats under full sail. Five yards farther on were the Pygmy huts, in a dark semi-circle open on our side. It was a quiet scene. The men and the women with their sleeping children ate silently beside the fire. Jacques told me that the hunting had gone well that day, they had taken two *boloko* and a *n'gandi*. The storm had passed on, and tonight there would be singing and dancing.

We finished our meal—the *n'gandi* was excellent—and while we smoked Jacques outlined his plan for the filming: different types of Pygmies, with a commentary on their anatomical peculiarities, then life in the forest encampment, domestic activities, the children.

"Those children—they are really most amusing. I watched them yesterday from the observatory, but I couldn't get near them. When I tried, they began to cry, and that wasn't very popular with the mothers, as you can imagine."

Then the drums began. Jacques rose and I asked him:

"Do we wait to be invited?"

"Not at all. Come on. Mougounzi told me that we could come and go as we liked."

Already the women were seated round the fire. Two small boys were beating the drums, one with his fists and the other with two sticks. Some youngsters were sketching out a dance—it had the look of the sort of Pyrrhic dance one sees on a Greek vase, though without lance or shield. The little creatures leaped from one leg to the other, kicking the free leg high in the air. This piece of graceful equilibrium seemed to be peculiar to them, and performed only by children. While it went on, no men joined in.

Two hunters appeared and the boys dispersed. Jacques whispered:

"Dangawé and Ndoumba, the best drummers in the camp."

They each took a drum—hollowed from a single piece of wood and covered with an antelope skin—and tested it with the flat of their hands; one drum seemed to be slack and Dangawé adjusted the wedges. Taking the drumsticks they rolled out a rapid, highly rhythmic measure and all the population of the camp began to gather round. Mougounzi appeared, to shake our hands, and sat down at our side. Old Télé gave me a grave nod of the head, and I returned his salute.

As the singing began I felt again the sensation of wonder of the first night. The choir lifted the whole community on a strong, calm wave. The basic plain-song, seemingly undirected, broke out in bursts of improvisation in which the individual contribution overtook the chorus, to be submerged in its turn in the ensemble. The voices of the men and the women were now the rumble of thunder, now the rustle of the rain, now the song of birds after the storm.

Never in my life did I hear a harmony in which a noble sentiment seemed so profoundly to mingle with and derive from a deep, cosmic natural richness.

Chapter VI

THE camp awoke. It was perhaps six o'clock; my
watch had stopped. The dawn crept through the
shadows of the forest and touched our clearing. Suddenly a cock crowed and I saw him there, mounted on a
hut, imposing in his immaculate plumage. How did he
come to be so grand and fat, I wondered, when all the
poultry we had ever seen or eaten up to now had been so
scrawny? Jacques, climbing into his shirt, told me
that the alarum-cock was a present from Motozélé. It
moved around the camp plundering all day, and the
Pygmies allowed it to scavenge after their meals.

Mougounzi came to shake hands again, and asked
Leonard whether we would accompany them on the
day's hunt, but Jacques said there was still work to do
around camp; moreover, he wanted to get the Pygmies
gradually used to the camera.

"Before you go running round the woods," I said,
"I'd like to have a look at your feet. You went to bed
early last night, and Trotty says you weren't well."

"That's true. I took some jiggers out of my feet, but
I was a bit late doing it, and the sores don't seem to
heal."

After breakfast I made him soak his feet in a permanganate solution while I prepared dressings and

sulphonamides. I did not like the look of his sores; the big toe of his right foot alone had eight suppurating little holes.

"If you don't want to finish your film in Ouesso hospital you had better be careful of these. We shall dress them every morning, and today you'd better lie up as long as possible."

Then I went back to see the hunters off. In groups of two and three they moved away, each with a net or an axe on his shoulder. As he passed from the huts into the forest old Télé roused a little yellow and white dog which stretched, yawned, and trotted after him. There were three dogs in the camp, of no recognisable breed, and it seemed certain that they had been given by the Africans. They, and the cock, were the only domestic animals.

The small boys followed their fathers, the girls followed their mothers, who carried their newly-born babies on the rudimentary sling from their shoulders. The two- to five-year-olds who could walk, but not enough to follow the hunt, stayed behind under the care of the old woman Kolé and the lame man Bakembé. Bakembé had been hurt in a gorilla hunt, but he carried his game leg with philosophy and, while we remained, was confident of not running short of tobacco. Mougounzi had already gone; now his wife followed him, a basket on her back and a little girl in her arms. As she rose she gave a shrill, thin call of quite astonishing purity, and my admiration became amazement when, without drawing breath, she prolonged this call and modulated it from sharp to flat with an extraordinary virtuosity. She disappeared, and I was still considering her amazing skill when Trotty appeared, lifting his eyes enquiringly from the camera.

"You heard that?"

As he spoke it came again, fainter but still perfectly true, a wailing yodel from the forest. What more surprises had the Babinga for us? Already, since our first meeting, we had been astonished by the skill of their woodsmanship, the beauty of their singing, the ingenuity of their dances, and still we barely knew them.

As they left one by one for the hunt I took the opportunity of noting their physical characteristics.

With a longish torso, short legs and long arms, their average height seemed to be about four feet four or five for the men, and perhaps four feet for the women. They differed in several particulars from their neighbours the Pomo.

The Pygmy is not by any means a degenerated individual; the chest wall is large and well shaped, and though the hands are small the arms are strong; the heels project backwards; the legs are thin. Their colouring is generally a shade lighter than that of the other Africans, particularly in the children, varying from a yellow ochre to a brown. Their growth of hair on the body is more developed than is usual among Africans; several of them beside Mougounzi wore moustaches, and three others, including old Télé, were bearded. The men shaved their heads, retaining of their fine frizzled hair only a top-knot, a crest or a forelock. The women, too, had shaven skulls.

Alexandre had told me that the Pygmies were ugly; but was it not only that they were different, and that the unusual is usually disliked more than admired? The Pygmy skull, I found, was less elongated than that of the African; the jaws were slightly projecting, the chin occasionally retreating. Seen full-face—the most characteristic and disconcerting aspect of the Pygmy—

the nose is remarkably big, presenting the shape of an equilateral triangle. On the other hand their lips are less thick and protuberant than the African's. Their eyes, of all shades of brown, are large and open, with a constantly watchful expression. Their ears are graceful and well modelled; as I had noticed during the camp-changing the previous week, the Pygmies have extremely sharp hearing.

Trotty had erected the camera, Leonard prepared the accumulators, Jacques had got up. His plan was to set the apparatus in the middle of the clearing and to invite Bakembé—whom he had christened Quasimodo—to inspect the camp through the view-finder.

The camera was aimed at a hut lit by the slanting rays of the sun. Leonard went to find our lame friend, who was busy cooking a handful of maize while Didier photographed him. He needed no persuasion to approach the Arriflex, adjusted to his height, and stand beside Jacques, who showed him how to look through the view-finder. Bakembé, visibly amused, looked from one to the other of us with an expression that clearly said: "You are making fun of me." However, he took the camera and did as he was told. For a long time he examined the little huts so mysteriously captured in the curious instrument. When he had finished he showed no surprise whatever, and merely nodded his head in an approving way. The game both pleased and interested him, but even when Trotty connected the batteries and turned the motors of the camera, the sound of the engine left Bakembé totally indifferent.

I moved off and approached the old woman Kolé, who was crouched low, using a tiny iron blade to smooth the lianas with which doubtless she was going to make a basket. Beside her was a baby who observed me with a terrified expression, its lips trembling and nostrils quivering; very soon it began to squall. Kolé took it in her arms, giving me a look of some indignation, and I hastily offered her a spoonful of sugar which I had prepared in advance, put up in a leaf. The old woman tested it between the thumb and forefinger, and gave a pinch of it to the baby, who began to calm down. She gave me a difficult smile. With her shaven head and disdainful forehead, her sunken cheeks, her prominent lower lip and her sunken eyes, she reminded me of some bust of a Roman emperor of the decadent period. Placing the child on the ground, where it lay happily blowing bubbles, she paid no more attention to me and continued to scrape her liana.

But Bakembé was working. His job was to stretch the skins of the beasts killed during the last few days; he took flexible rods of wood and attached the skins to them so that they might be cured in the sun. Trotty and Jacques had filmed the process in detail. As a result Bakembé was able to add another two leaves of tobacco to the hoard in the box he kept hidden in the leaves of his roof. This was the place in which he concealed all his most precious possessions: a few phosphorus matches, two cigarettes and a little tobacco. He also showed me, with a lifting of the head and a raising of the eyebrows—a familiar gesture—a bracelet: a very simple affair of three pieces of wood threaded on a string.

Two yards away a little boy, less frightened than the rest, was studying my movements. I motioned towards him, and at once he darted back to rejoin three little fellows playing with branches in a patch of sunshine.

93

Another one nearby was gathering up grains of maize and eating them. That gave me an idea: if we could only manage to tame the children, we should have no more trouble with the women.

I went back to our quarters and, gathering up all the grains I could find, I filled an old jam pot. Dominique came with me, and very gravely and silently we approached the camp, and sat down a few yards from the children. We began to play with the plump, yellow grains, letting them fall from one hand to the other, the children watching the performance with envious eyes. To help the process, Dominique threw some of the grains towards them, making sure they fell in the open ground between them and ourselves. Two children risked approaching them: one walked upright, the other came on all fours. They had only to stretch out an arm to take the stuff from our open hands. In a moment every child had its mouth full, and it was necessary to make a distribution to the smallest ones as well. After all this old Kolé, who had been watching every movement, took courage and approached too. I was exceedingly sorry, but the pot was now empty. Dominique showed her, but she continued to insist— what she wanted was just the pot itself. He presented it to her; she took it and darted into the hut to conceal her treasure.

By the afternoon the sky was overcast, greatly to the distress of Jacques, who would not be able to film the return of the hunters. Heavy clouds began to collect over the forest; surely there would be a tornado in the evening. Before long the Babenzélé began to hurry home and Jacques, stretched again on his bed, observed that they no longer sang. Leonard, who had been talking with Dangawé, reported that they had taken only one *boloko*, so they would not be able to give us any meat that day. When Mougounzi arrived, he had a preoccupied air. I asked him what was the matter and he pointed a finger to the sky, nodded his head and replied briefly, "*M'bwa*."

"M'sieu", said Leonard, "he says: 'Rain.'"

The women had revived the embers of the fire, and began to prepare the big meal of the day. The division of the one and only animal was quick enough; there was not to be much meat tonight, so it was a good thing that there was some manioc left. The camp, uneasy before the storm, began to settle down; already the children were in the huts and the men had packed away the nets and the spears. In a curiously violent fashion the crickets began to sing their metallic song. Not a branch stirred; under a sky heavy with clouds the forest lay there, immobile, almost silent.

Didier had gone to see if our gear was all right while Trotty emptied the magazine of the camera; because of the extreme humidity it was not a good thing to keep exposed film there overnight. Sitting in our shelter I jotted down the main events of the day. "Saturday, 31st August, Babenzélé camp, in the forest: One difficulty: Jacques' feet are in a deplorable state. Initiated Bakembé into the mysteries of the camera; then filmed him preparing skins. Fed the children. . . ."

A sudden squall of wind lifted the mosquito-nets; the leaves were abruptly torn away, the insects became all of a sudden mute. A huge drop of water fell on my page, followed in quick succession by others. Five o'clock, and the storm was on its way, in a hurry. The claps of thunder came faster and faster, with an increasing and almost terrible violence; great waves of violet lightning illumined our clearing. The rain now fell completely, wholly, vertically. There never was rain like it. At the foot of our beds a curtain of water fell from the pent-roof—but not a single drop penetrated the thick phrynium-leaf tiles. Now and again we glanced towards our neighbours. At the start of the storm they had vanished each man into his hut, with fathers taking their children on their knees to comfort them, the mother blowing gently on a burning brand she had saved from the downpour. They stared out philosophically at the deluge, showing not the slightest apprehension as the thunderclaps reverberated through the forest.

The storm passed eventually, following the course of the Sangha. As the rain slackened we threw "ponchos" over our shoulders—the rubber squares of the British Army—and ran towards the big tent. Pascal and Bernard had taken the remainder of our bread and made sandwiches. We had strictly forbidden any lighting of fires inside, because of risk to the film, but Leonard had made a special shelter under which he had managed to boil some water. Proudly, he served us some tea, and very grateful we were for it, since the storm had reduced the surrounding temperature by many degrees; we were glad of our sweaters too. The rain had stopped, but it still dripped heavily from the trees above us. We ate quietly enough in our shelter.

Suddenly, between mouthfuls, I stopped and listened. Over the camp grew a vague, curious sound. "Hush." We stopped our meal to listen. The silence, interrupted only by the sound of heavy drops of water falling on leaves, was extraordinary. We began to eat again—and there again was the sound. "Leonard," murmured somebody.

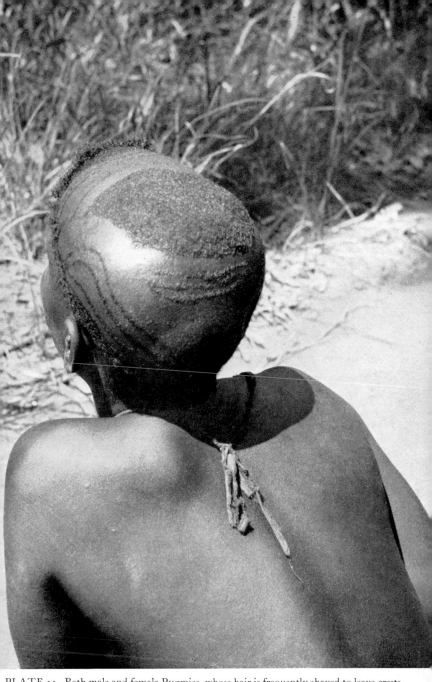

PLATE 11. Both male and female Pygmies, whose hair is frequently shaved to leave crests or topknots, sometimes adopt this exotic form, produced with the blades of machetes or knives sharpened on a stone.

PLATE 12. Babenzélé Pygmies: Jacques Dupont and his interpreter (*right*) have gathered the Pygmies round the microphone. One can recognise (*reading from left to right*) Bakembé, Ndilo and Mougounzi, the camp-leader.

Pascal replied, "He isn't there."

Nobody spoke, because now we could hear a voice growing gradually louder, with an increasing emphasis. We rose, and at that moment, unhurriedly, in came Leonard.

"What goes on?"

"It's nothing. Télé—the old one with the beard—he is making rain-prayers."

He meant: prayers to distract the rain, to drive it off. We made a rush towards this scene; over the sodden footpath we made no sound, but it was too late. In the camp nothing moved, nothing stirred. Only the hut of Mougounzi was lit by a burning lump of resin on a wand of wood. Njaoué, his wife, lay on a bark bed with her baby at her breast. And Mougounzi, Télé and Dangawé, his neighbours, were talking together very quietly.

The showers fell abruptly, intermittently. The dawn came grey and dank and cold. The Babenzélé were in no hurry to get up, and neither were we. We dressed slowly—for the Pygmies the business of rising was a simple question of leaving their hut. Leonard said:

"They won't go hunting. The rain is still on the trees."

Even if the sun appeared at noon it would be too late; a few hours of sun would never dry off this sodden forest. But why, I wondered, would they not hunt after the rain? Surely they could not be afraid of getting wet? Still—if they stayed in the camp we could make use of them; given a little luck and a ray of sun, we could possibly do some photography.

Jacques and I sat ourselves on some drums of wood in the driest spot we could find. Leonard stayed with us, since we never knew when we might need his help. According to him, the rains had barely begun. As for the film men, the question was whether there would be time for them to take anything at all. I tried to console them:

"Come on—sufficient unto the day. . . . In any case we haven't any choice. In the dry season you never see the sun at all. We have storms, but we may also have sun."

At least, in the last twenty-four hours, the condition of Jacques' feet had greatly improved. Nevertheless, we kept up the treatment.

Right in front of us, not in the least embarrassed by our presence, five little Pygmies were playing like children play the world over; they were amusing themselves in a puddle with little boats of bark. I recognised two of the babies who had taken our grain the other day; another, a little older, had doubtless been out hunting. Leonard asked his name:

"Atata," he said, timidly.

Jacques, with his pencil and pad ready, scratched his chin and declared, "These children have a terrific vitality. They run about naked, and this humidity and rain and heat doesn't seem to worry them at all. They don't even get colds."

"Probably. But did you ever think of how many, of all this crowd here, ever reach maturity—adulthood? And look at the fifty-odd people of this camp—how many of them are really old? You know the one with the beard——?"

"Télé?"

"Yes—and the other, my decadent Roman emperor, old Kolé, the one who loves jam—— But here's another."

Before us passed an old woman we had not seen before—bent double, leading a little girl who could not have been more than six. She was noticeable, the little one, because of her troubled expression and the difficult way in which she limped on her heels, her head bowed on her shoulders.

"Leonard, take this cigarette, give it to the old girl and ask her to come here."

Leonard did as he was told, and reported: "She says she is the little one's grandmother. The mother is dead. She says she badly needs medicine for the child."

The old one's name was Ongonié, the child Kounié. Her feet were wretched, covered with vast sores, a terrible case of the jigger insect. As for the old woman, her eyes were inflamed by who knew what infection; great tears coursed down the wrinkles of her face. Was she blind, I wondered momentarily. No; I offered her another cigarette, and she reached for it with a hand like a mummy's. If we could do nothing for the old woman, at least we might possibly help the child.

I dived into the medicine-chest and applied the same remedies as I had used on Jacques. When the child cried, Jacques tried to console her with a little jam. The treatment was not exactly useless, but I had no great hopes of its success; the trouble was greatly advanced and I felt I needed the help of Hartweg, who would soon be with us. The little girl went on her painful way, and sat down beside Njaoué, the chief's wife.

Njaoué, in front of her hut, was preoccupied with the manufacture of a vast carrying-basket, her baby across her lap. Now and again it reached for her breast and fed. Like all the Pygmy women—except the very young and the very old—she wore a tight cord around the root of the breasts, incurably distorting them. Her fingers moved nimbly among the fibres she was using. I decided to try and talk to her as soon as Alexandre returned, but it seemed pointless to interrupt her now, as she worked industriously on, never pausing in her work except to shift the baby to a more convenient position.

The sky cleared, the sun suddenly glanced through the trees, and Jacques hurried back to prepare the cameras.

A little later, as the humidity evaporated, a group of children moved into the forest, and with them went a young, firm-breasted girl. Their job was to find the caterpillars which, they hoped, would have tumbled from the trees. When they came back their baskets were full, and I was amazed to see with how many varieties. Didier and Jacques hurried to photograph them, asking them to stand with their harvest in a patch of sunlight. There were little pale-green caterpillars with supple, bright-red extremities, others with black-and-yellow bands. The green ones were those we had tried at Kombo-Kombo, the Baya village, and I recognised the bigger orange ones as those which had diverted Joachim in the canoe. There were brown, hairy ones, rolling themselves into shapes resembling in miniature the hats of Russian noblemen.

The young girl, Kenié, sat down on a log surrounded by babies. She began to sort out the caterpillars, and Leonard explained: "The green ones are for drying and smoking, the big ones are for cooking in boiling water."

Kenié took some of the silken cocoons and, with a deft gesture, tore them open and expelled the rosy naked caterpillars into a basket. By and by she added a few embers, shook the whole thing vigorously about and then turned out the caterpillars, done to a turn. Little hands stretched out for the delicious morsels; the cameras rolled. The feast went on some time and very soon the small faces were shining with grease; there was enough for everyone.

One shy little girl took refuge in the shadow of a hut, with three great hairy caterpillars writhing in her hand. I followed her, curious to see what she would do with them. Would she just eat them raw? Between her thumb and forefinger she took one of them, skewered it on a piece of bamboo, and skinned it in the twinkling of an eye; the oily yellow juice she carefully drained into a rolled up leaf. The others were similarly treated, then salted and put in a safe place to be savoured at leisure. . . .

Chapter VII

Jungle Surgery — The Making of Baskets — The End of a Hunt — The Girl-Man — Hunting by Nets — Sharing the Kill.

THUNDER growled in the darkness; it was not yet midnight. At intervals the lightning illuminated our mosquito-nets. The rain cascaded on to our beds, drenching us. Dominique turned over, swearing; Jacques cursed the cock, which he had seen destroying our leaf-roof.

"*He'll* finish up in the pot," said Didier.

But soon the rain stopped. A good thing too, because we hoped to go hunting the next day.

Rouget had been with us for the past two days. Before coming to us he had been to the camp of the Bangombé Pygmies, where we would surely have some work to do; he hoped to keep them patiently waiting until we had finished with the Babenzélé. Nief and Hartweg had come to see us too, giving us news of Pierre, who was staying at Gatongo, doing a portrait of Motozélé. Hartweg wanted to go north as far as possible, following the line of the Sangha, studying all the various races and tribes, moving from village to village. He spent part of his time with us attending to the children. As for little Kounié, he did not conceal the fact that there was nothing much one could do for her.

"There's a risk of spreading the infection. It needs

some surgery too delicate for us to chance, and treatment with the penicillin which we haven't got. It's possible that the sores may close up themselves and the inflammation die down by degrees. This business of natural-selection eliminates the weaker subjects, and these children have an exceptional resistance."

"But these jiggers—it's curious that they do nothing to remove them."

"I know, it's extraordinary, especially as the other Africans know perfectly well how to get rid of them."

Hartweg was, however, able to relieve many infected sores, caused by a skin parasite, which produced intense itching, exacerbated by their scratching. It was evident that the Pygmy hygiene was very rudimentary.

Meanwhile Jacques and his men went to film the making of the cords of which the Babenzélé construct their hunting-nets. They used big aluminium-covered screens to act as reflectors in the half-light of the forest. Ndoumba was sitting before a hank of long fibres, which Dangawé had made supple by striking it against a tree. With one hand Ndoumba rolled a length against his thigh while the other separated the strands before twisting them. After the preliminary twisting the first string is again twisted with another, and so on to the thickness of cord required. I asked Alexandre what was the red powder they applied to their thighs before rolling the strings.

"It is the earth from an ant-hill, burned and ground down. We, the Pomo, we use it too for string-making. And the fibres? You see those sticks drying in the sun— that is the kosa liana. We use it for our fibres too."

"Then it was the Pomo who taught the Pygmies?"

"No, that was the Yassoua. They taught us too."

We continued our researches with Njaoué, the wife of Mougounzi, who listened courteously to my questions, put through Alexandre. We talked of fire. Before they knew matches (which everyone in the district, Pygmies included, call *fofolo*, a corruption of the Spanish *fosforos*) the Pygmies made fire by twirling a stick of soft wood against a hard one, a process which was still understood by the older ones, but nowadays they used matches provided by the Pomo. I had noticed before, however, that the Pygmies took great care of their fire, and it was always someone's duty to see that at least one fire was always maintained and kept alive with slow-burning fuel. When they moved, they took it with them; conventionally the woman's task.

When storms broke they would move the fire into a hut, or at least out of the rain. They dug no hole and made no hearth; for activating the fire they used nothing but their own breath. Alexandre told me that they used their fire for no other purpose than cooking; they knew nothing of metallurgy or forging, nor of pottery, and they made no canoes. The other Africans would occasionally burn stretches of forest for their cultivation, but not so the Pygmies, having no agriculture. In these explanations of Alexandre's I detected, from the tone of his voice, the slight contempt in which he still held the Pygmies. I remembered his early astonishment at our wanting to know them at all.

Were they in fact dirty? Certainly they never washed, or rarely; they had not enough water and no kind of soap. Were they ugly? No; their build was on normal human lines, and if "they smelled bad" it had not incommoded us, being chiefly the smell of wood-smoke that impregnates the clothes of European charcoal-burners and, with the Pygmies, clung to their skin.

Mougounzi came and sat by, full of curiosity, his gaze moving to my face when I spoke, and to my hand when I took notes. The process of writing seemed to be one more peculiar charm to add to the magic of our machinery.

Now we spoke of basket-making, with Njaoué tranquilly answering questions while she nursed her child. The baby was asleep, and we spoke softly. Basket-making, it seemed, was the work of women and even of quite small girls. At Alexandre's request Njaoué had ranged round her all the types of basket used by the Babenzélé women. I greatly admired one big carrying-basket some three feet high and two feet across, very finely woven, in a diamond-shaped pattern. Round the opening it was decorated with a pleasant trefoil design of extremely flexible canes. The harness and the head-band, of supple bark, were held by little handles woven into the body of the basket. Both sturdy and graceful on the backs of these strong little women, the baskets were used as removal-vans and as caravans for the forest gypsies.

The smaller baskets were of the same pattern as the big ones, and Njaoué let me see the one she was in the process of making. The base was a woven square the projections of which were carried up to make the fundamental architecture of the frame. As she approached the top the weaver made use of a hoop of bark to hold the web together. Then she showed me a pannier woven in a beautiful straw, with bell-shaped sides, and a strainer of very fine mesh. Alexandre murmured:

"The basket for the prepared manioc and the sieve for the flour; it was the Gatongo women who make them for the Babinga. We the Pomo give them so much, so much, so much; you will see that, Monsieur Noël."

So we pursued our work without too much disturbing the life of the camp. That morning we filmed the departure for the hunt, and even if some detail was still missing, the greater part was in the can. Dangawé and old Télé had been the most intelligent and helpful performers, following the patches of light indicated by Jacques and walking exactly where they were told. In one shot Dangawé had seized his spear in his left hand to reach for a whistle with his right; when we re-took this he observed, without prompting, that he must hold his weapon as he had done before. Old Télé, as usual, roused his dog with the butt of his spear; the dog stretched and yawned, and man and beast disappeared into the undergrowth in the most natural way imaginable, without a glance at the camera, paying no attention to our presence, to the reflectors, to the sound of the motor.

At the end of the afternoon Mounika, the chorus-master, returned to camp with the others carrying a *n'gandi* on his shoulders. He hung it on a tree and began to skin it, using a very sharp knife, removing the hide with the greatest skill. Jacques asked if he might have it, in exchange for some salt and tobacco.

"No, Monsieur Jacques, the hide doesn't belong to the Babenzélé. The skins belong to Motozélé. The Hausa takes them."

"What Hausa?"

"See, Monsieur Noël—the Babinga kill the animals in the forest, they keep the meat and give some to Motozélé, and Motozélé gets the skins. He sells them to the Hausa merchant who comes by and collects all the hides."

I turned to Jacques: "These hide-dealers are the

Mohammedan traders of the region; if you start competing with them you'll put up the price."

Alexandre, who had heard the last part of the sentence, interposed: "Ah, no, for you the price is always the same, the price of friends."

The flayed carcass of the antelope looked enormous against its fragile hooves. Its tendons stood out finely, the muscles seemed strong. With its coat no more than a pile of hair on the ground the creature still looked vigorous, almost graceful. Mounika pressed a large-bladed knife on the animal's belly, and said something, nodding.

"What did he say, Alexandre?"

"The baby is still inside."

Mounika opened the beast from the tail to the sternum and eviscerated it carefully, throwing the entrails on to a large leaf; then he removed the foetus in its mother-of-pearl-coloured covering. He hung it on a branch. Alexandre, with a slightly repelled air, confided to me:

"They will hang it in the smoke and cure it. Soft meat—they like it."

There came the far-away sound of chanting, one or two voices raised above the chorus, and shrill cries: the arrival of the hunters. Mounika began to sharpen his knives, and Alexandre said: "When they sing, they have had a good day."

At that moment they arrived, men, women and children coming back into the last rays of the sun cutting obliquely through the leaves. Dangawé and Ndoumba had a *boloko* each. The camp that had been almost deserted all day began to teem again with life, while the smoke from the cooking fires climbed into the vault of the trees.

Four days had passed since I had come back with Didier, eight since the arrival of the film men. How many more days would we need in the forest? The Pygmies intended to return to their base camp at the end of the week, and there would be no changing their minds for them. We had no time to lose. Jacques, now cured, was anxious to accompany the Pygmies on a hunting expedition.

Trotty and Didier took some shots of the rope-making, with Moboma, Ndilo and Bakaé stripping the strands of kosa that had been drying over the fire. The first time we saw Bakaé we took him for a girl; he was the son of Mounika but he had the breast of a woman. This clearly embarrassed him; we saw how he tried to undertake all the heavier tasks to prove his virility. Leonard and Alexandre assured us that he was a male, but we were unsure what to call him in view of his anatomical peculiarity.

The stripped lianas were split lengthwise, and the Pygmies manipulated the ends by holding them between their toes or on a small fork. With a knife they then scraped out the fibres, which were hung up in hanks to dry.

As the hunters went off in groups we followed Mougounzi and Dangawé. The women were on the march too, and from time to time there rang out the strange piercing yodel, echoing into the vault of the trees. Only a few steps from the camp and we were lost in the mass of vegetation and undergrowth. We had some difficulty keeping up with our guides, who travelled fast, too fast for us in that tangle of roots and branches.

Some way on we met Njaoué, Kenié and two other women. I followed them. Njaoué and one of the others still bore their babies in the shoulder-cradle, which left their arms free. They rummaged here and there like hens in a farmyard, picking up fruits and vegetables, several varieties of nut, wild potatoes and mangoes. The basket of Kenié was nearly full when she cried out: "Kongo! Kongo!"

A column of caterpillars was proceeding along a fallen tree—the green kind that the Pygmies dry and smoke. Once again Njaoué uttered her strange, almost unhumanly piercing call, and from some way off another answered it. We approached each other, and by and by in a narrow clearing I found everyone gathered together. Jacques was full of high spirits.

"Leonard and Dangawé have been superb!" he said, "especially Dangawé." The Pygmy knew we were talking of him, and looked proud. "He kept all the action in the patches of light with consummate art. They are first-rate actors."

We had arrived at the hunting-ground selected in advance by old Télé and another veteran, who wore an ancient blue cap. "How did Ndékoué come by that hat?" I asked.

"The police hat? Why, it was the old chief of the Pomo, Motozélé's father, who gave it to him years ago." My question appeared to have caused surprise.

Atata lit the fire with the smoking brand he had carried with him all morning. Njaoué put the wild tubers to cook in the cinders. Other women broke open the heavy stones of the wild mangoes for the nut inside, yet others prepared the caterpillars. Mangazou, a lively lad with an alert eye, had spotted a huge spiral snail in a hole of a tree, with a shell bigger than his fist. He dug the creature out with a stick and began to grill it at the fire. Everyone shared everything. The picnic went on in the silent business of eating.

We had intended to content ourselves with a head of corn each and a tin of condensed milk, but Mougounzi offered us almonds and wild potatoes. They were not bad. The roots reminded me of a Jerusalem artichoke, and the nuts were rather like those of apricots. A little girl sat down beside us and offered us some fruit in the form of little red balls, in bunches like grapes. They were very sweet, and usually reserved for children.

The pause was not long. Smoking a cigarette, I examined the blades of the axes and spears. The workmanship was clumsy, without decoration except for some vague striation on the blades. Logoué explained:

"It is Taba, the chief of the Gatongo, who makes these things for the Pomo and the Babenzélé, in exchange for skins and meat."

The blades were attached to the hafts with cords covered with a thick, black pitch, a sort of resin mixed with earth. The point of the spears ended in a socket and was rammed straight on to the staff, but the axe heads were wedged and morticed. The axe handles were billets of wood, heavy enough at the other end to serve also as a mallet.

At a sign from Télé and Mougounzi, silence fell on the company. Didier took the Eyemo out of its case, Trotty passed him the tins of film, the camera was loaded. The women and children would wait here for the hunters, who rose and, in utter silence, moved off, with ourselves behind them, trying also to make no sound. All traces of dew had gone; now the heat of the sun began to strike through the trees, but it was rare indeed that any direct ray of light fell on the stealthy column of hunters, as they advanced through this strange green light where all movements seemed slowed and all sounds stifled.

We halted for a while, and Ndoumba and Dangawé went off to scout for the gazelle. Hardly five minutes had passed when they returned, and each one led off a file of hunters, one to the left and another to the right. The nets were now to be placed to surround the game. Each net measured nearly fifty yards long; attached by a wooden hook to the fork of a branch and anchored to the ground by a root, it presented a barrier about a yard high. When all was ready, there was a circle, yielding yet impenetrable, nearly half a mile in circumference. During all this operation not a branch had cracked, scarcely a leaf moved, not a word been uttered. As the minutes ticked by in silence I heard the two monotonous notes of some woodland bird and the murmur of a stream nearby.

With a bound Mounika leaped into the enclosure, seized a branch and began to beat the underbrush, shouting. More shouts broke out on all sides; more hunters began to beat and thrash the forest, while others remained on the lookout beyond the net, their lances ready for the animals. The forest resounded with shouts and barks; it became hard to distinguish the cries of the men from those of the dogs.

Didier and Dupont were the next to clear the net, followed by Trotty with the film. Five yards in front of them a big *n'gandi* waited in a clump of bushes, the colour of his coat mingling with the dusk. Suddenly he leaped forward and again stopped, immobile. Didier, his eye to the finder, turned the camera—one, two, three seconds and the creature had seen them and was away. More cries broke out ahead, and we found ourselves watching a *boloko* which had hurled itself into the net. In a moment the delicate hues of his flanks were covered with blood, and in another moment he was

111

dead. Atata gave a shout of triumph. Even among the children the instinct welled up, the instinct of the chase, the necessity to kill to live, the need to be warier than the beast, and stronger too.

A dog yelped, there was another great rustling of foliage, and a *n'gandi* bounded by, a few yards away. It could have been the same *n'gandi*, but his movements were less nimble; he was wounded in the haunch. Mougounzi was after him, followed by Ndoumba, and we followed them both. My foot caught in a root. I was down and up almost in one movement. Didier caught his trouser-leg in a projection. Bakaé and Mounika came up on the right; Ndékoué and two more Pygmies rushed to cut off the retreat of the animal, which threw itself in desperation against the net. It bent, but resisted; the *n'gandi* made a half-turn, but one of his back legs and his little antlers were held by the meshes. Dangawé, waiting outside the barrier, caught him full in the breast with his spear. He struggled only until Mougounzi finished him off with the flat of his axe on the skull. Then, hoisting him on his back, Dangawé set off alone for the camp.

It was all over now. The women had rejoined us; the men packed the nets. It was perhaps three in the afternoon, and we began to return, following another invisible track. The performance began again. The nets were laid—but this time without luck; a couple of *boloko* escaped just as the circle was closing on them.

When this had happened twice, a curious ceremony was prepared. Old Télé, who was doubtless considered the veteran hunter, collected the Pygmies at the base of a tree and then, with a liana, bound several leaves round the trunk, while he called, one after another, the names of the animals of the forest. Each name was

PLATE 13. Babenzélé Pygmies at home.

PLATE 14. The Babenzélé use the long fibres of liana to spin the cords with which they make their hunting-nets.

accompanied by a long-drawn cry of "Heeee—" from the crowd.

After a brief silence Télé slashed the liana with a blow from his machete, while the hunters gave a loud shout followed by a phrase I was not able to note at the time, but which was later explained to me by Alexandre as meaning: "Yes, we are glad!" He told me that the "Apependo", the magic rite, was designed to propitiate the forest spirits and to increase the game in the nets. The Pomo did the same thing, he said, when the hunting was going badly.

That evening the photography was finished. The sun sank and the shadows invaded the forest. The hunters paused at the edge of a stream, and while the men and children entered the water the women continued their walking. We bathed too, though there was not enough water for swimming. The clear, tepid water was refreshing after the day's fatigue; we washed away the mud and the blood from the thorns. The Pygmies played, splashing, but we moved along the stream a little way until we found a place where it was deep enough even to dive. Alarmed, three ducks flew racketing away.

The Babinga did not come with us. Logoué explained that they are frightened of holes in the river. They cannot swim, they cannot make canoes, they never catch big fish—sometimes the women net little inshore tiddlers in their baskets, but nothing is ever caught from deep water. The Pygmies are not waterfolk, at best they stay in the shallows.

Back in camp the kill from the hunt was shared out. Dangawé had skinned the *n'gandi* and the *boloko* very skilfully and dismembered them. A dog sniffed hungrily around the pieces laid out on a tray made of twigs.

Mougounzi presided over the distribution. The man who had first struck the animal was first served; he could make his choice of the cuts, but all got equal shares however much or little there was. The fires were lit. Njaoué took away the guts in a pot, Mounika's wife got the ribs, Dangawé's a shoulder. The old woman Kolé went on whining until she was given the *boloko's* head. When all was done Mougounzi came up and begged a cigarette from me, with a most effective imitative gesture, the fingers to the lips. For the first time I noticed that his right ear was pierced with a hole big enough to carry his home-made cigarette-holder carved from a stick.

Everyone broke into little groups for dinner, sitting on the ground each with a large leaf as a plate, eating slowly. If a baby cried its mother quickly gave it the breast, or slipped a piece of cooked banana between its lips. The meat was generally boiled, and the Pygmies ate it kneading in the fingers knobs of manioc or maize flour. Nobody spoke; it was all most simple and dignified; everyone took the portion assigned to him, nor did anyone look enviously at his neighbour's share. The night came swiftly down.

Chapter VIII

*Nearly a Fire — Mounika Dances — Dance of the Women
— The Invasion of Ants — Preparing for the Elephant.*

MOUGOUNZI had offered us a haunch of the
n'gandi, although it was fair to say we had probably impeded the hunters more than helped them. We
were glad to accept it, since now there was only a handful of rice left to share with Leonard and Pascal. We
hoped for reprovisioning next day; Alexandre had
taken a letter to Nief asking for rice, sugar, oil and
coffee.

Before dinner Trotty had carefully sorted out the
reels of exposed film. We had now enough to pack one
case, and Didier prepared the soldering-lamp, so that
the film could be encased in zinc—the "tropical pack"
so necessary in such humidity. The preservation of the
film worried us quite a lot, and Trotty enclosed with it
not only absorbent pastilles but yards of toilet paper
he had dried in front of the fire in an old pot. We had
bought great quantities of these rolls from the Greek
trader in Ouesso, much to his astonishment; we had
given him no explanation as to why we should need
such unusual numbers. To begin with we had considered using rice, dried in the same manner, to reduce
the humidity in the tins, but already it was clear we
needed it to eat.

All the tins were ready; Didier lit his lamp and
watched the thin streak of lead that was closing up the

joints. "We're lucky to get this tin closed," he said. "What a firework show it could have been——"

Jacques interrupted caustically, "I asked Leonard not to light fires in the tent. Seems he was cold after the rain. What an idea—to use the paraffin from the storm-lamp! A good job we noticed, or what a show— all the new film and the work of a week. As though we hadn't enough troubles with this damned sun."

"We won't see much more of it. This evening the sky was grey all over; we're more likely in for a storm."

"As though last night's shower-bath wasn't enough."

"First a flood, then a possible conflagration. Is this a circus?"

"Never mind," said Jacques, "after this day's work, it's bed for us all at nine."

Happily there was a little tea left. The water from the stream a hundred yards away was undrinkable without a lot of permanganate, which was far from pleasant. We had given up the idea of filtering it; one needed to watch a filter all day to get a cup of pure water, which, in any case, still tasted strongly of vege-table decomposition. By brewing it into tea it was possible to disguise it.

Mougounzi came to see us. We offered him one of our last cigarettes and gave him his own greeting: "*Omouviako*." This is a good word, meaning neither "Good morning" nor "Good evening", but signifying simply: "You're here."

When the drums began to throb he rose, and we followed him. In spite of our fatigue it was always delightful to share their fire among the leaping shadows of the forest, to hear the songs and watch the dance.

The singing was occasionally accompanied by hand-clapping or the rhythmic beating of sticks. Mounika

used a rattle made of a little basket half full of nuts,
Ndilo banged an old gong of beaten iron presented by
the Pomo.

Mounika, Mougounzi and Mboma rose and began
to dance; they jumped from one foot to another, their
muscles tensed, their arms along the length of their
bodies. A fourth man joined them, then two more, then
Bakaé, in spite of his woman's breasts. This dance,
"Djoboko," is reserved for men. The drum-beat became very fast, the men's muscles fluttered on their
chests. The dancers revolved around the fire, advanced
in a line and stood, quivering with that characteristic
vibration which I never saw at any time in Africa other
than among the Pygmies. Mounika clapped his hands
and the whole company followed him, chanting *allegro*,
punctuating it with high calls from the women and the
children.

The drum-beat began to accelerate even more; the
sweat streaked down the bodies of Dangawé and
Ndoumba, whose actions grew faster too, achieving a
sort of frenetic tattoo with their heels on the earth.
They held their arms in front of their knees, and their
feet began to describe a movement like that of skaters
going backwards. The choreography was tremendously
rapid, but also quite controlled, and not even in the
paroxysm of the dance did the Pygmies allow themselves to be overtaken by the kind of collective delirium
often seen among the Africans.

The rhythm slackened; one by one the dancers returned to sit among the spectators. At last Mounika
alone was left, walking across the arena beating his
hands. The song died away quietly on a bass note
hummed by the men with closed lips.

Conversation broke out again, with the women

praising the virtuosity of the drummers, the grace of Mougounzi, the skill of the chorus-master. A mother hoisted up a baby which, in her attention to the dance, had slipped between her legs. The little children began to chase each other, falling among people's legs, picking themselves up laughing. The fathers grabbed them with an affectionate pat on the cheek or the shoulder—but there was never a kiss; never even among wives and husbands, mothers and children, do the Pygmies kiss. They do not appear to know how.

Bakaé threw some wood on the fire. Then, to the same chant, but without drums, the women began to dance.

I remembered that on the day of our arrival Mougounzi had called on one of the women to perform. He had been obliged to insist, and even old Télé's help had been enlisted to persuade her. When at last she stood up she seemed seized with embarrassment, and held her hand to her face as though to avoid some awful sight. Now and again she would open her mouth, but no sound came forth. It seemed clear that we had been the cause of her distress. A murmur, either of protest or of fear, had come from the crowd, and in a moment she was back among them, with Mounika tactfully starting a new song.

Jacques said to me now:

"The second time I came to their evening, when I was alone with them, Mougounzi had to ask several times for a volunteer. A woman got up and tried out some halting steps, lifting her hands awkwardly over her head. Then she ran back. Everyone laughed at her."

But tonight we caused them no fear. Three women rose, but, since the "Djanga" is an individual dance, they performed one by one. They were accompanied by a slow, heavily-figured chant. The dancer turned on herself as she moved around the fire—successively facing the spectators, the fire, another turn and so on. She carried her arms now over her head and now at her waist. It was an improvisation based on all the inflections of the singing, an inspirational thing.

The first two dancers perfectly understood the effects of surprise. They took several steps towards the audience, only to turn abruptly away and then, with a sudden whirl, face the crowd again; they would make several hesitant half-turns finishing up with a dramatic figure at an unexpected moment. The star of the evening was certainly Njaoué, who not only had a superb natural spontaneity but showed a great ironic sense in her mime, her gestures of limbs and expression. The song was punctuated with bursts of laughter. Then suddenly Njaoué returned to her place and took back her baby from the hands of the old woman Ongonié.

The party was over and everyone began to go back to the huts, where already several babies had been put to sleep on little beds of bark, stripped off the tree in single pieces about a yard long. We, too, went back to our leaf hut, which we had covered with a tarpaulin against the rain, in case the camp cockerel should decide to use us for his perch.

We had not been long in bed when Didier—in the next cot to me, nearest to the forest—reached in his pocket, scratched a match and said, "Hey—look at this!"

"What's going on?" asked Trotty indifferently.

"Just an invasion of ants, that's all."

We all jumped up together. Trotty lit the lamp and directed its beam on to the ground. A great column of insects, in tight ranks several yards wide, flowed across the ground like a sort of liquid, among the dead leaves, thrusting aside the twigs and bits of debris that stood in their way. For several seconds we watched them silently, motionless, almost stupefied; I distinctly heard the curious rustling of millions of miniature yet sinister feet; the crepitation of the questing antennae of this legion that pressed inexorably forward, at the command of some invisible general. Memories of old adventure stories came back to me: these ant-armies were no invention, for here was one before my eyes. One of them had already ventured on Didier's bed, crossed it and was down the other side. Others were beginning to climb on mine, on Dominique's. A few scouts had even started on Jacques', whose bed faced the Pygmy huts.

There was a sudden yelping from the end of the camp, and the horrified figure of the old woman Kolé appeared in our beam of light. She was jumping on one leg and shouting:

"*Yamou dindi, yamou dindi!*"

At that moment Logoué appeared, from his bed under the shelter.

"What does she say?"

"She says: 'Oh, her foot!'"

We went to the old woman, who kept pointing her finger downwards, calling: "*Mabmoko, mabmoko*—(the creatures)!"

This roused everyone. We shone our lamp on Kolé's hut—the ground was invaded by enormous black ants, the Soldier Ants whose powerful jaws had bitten her. She rushed to take shelter in the far-away hut of Ongonié. For the moment most of the camp was free from the attack; the columns of ants were passing to its left, though our shelter was in its path.

For ten minutes we beat the bushes with branches, hoping to disperse the invaders. It seemed to distract them only slightly. Reinforced by the great company behind them, the ants regrouped at once and pressed relentlessly forward—they slid through our sandals, climbed up our trousers, and bit us with such tenacity that it was necessary to tear them off by force. While this was going on Didier hurried off to find the soldering-lamp. Lighting it, he played the pale-blue flame on the columns of ants, interrupting their march. Twigs, leaves and ants were consumed; the earth itself got hot and the followers-on, manifestly upset, shrank back. Didier swung the lamp from left to right, grilling the ants in all directions. A bush began to burn.

In its light we observed two kinds of ants: the big black ones, almost half an inch long, the "fighters," which began to devour the second they attached themselves to living flesh, and the red ones, only half as big, which merely followed each other about, the "workers". Even in the face of our flame-thrower, once the first panic had passed, those ants not in its direct path continued endlessly to push ahead, bearing off their wounded, climbing over their dead.

Half an hour of this was enough for us; we retreated. Taking up our beds and nets, we shook off the stragglers, and retired under the big tent.

All night long the ants filed by. The camp itself was spared, except for the outside huts, whose occupants moved into the centre out of the line of march. It might be that the army did not dare advance over the open space beaten so flat by the dancers' feet, the games of the children and the daily life of the encampment.

Even by morning the last outriders of the ant army were still passing through the camp, across the previous night's battlefield where the last stragglers moved over the ashes. It was early afternoon before we were rid of them.

At ten in the morning the sky was leaden grey. After the disturbed night we rose late, and shared out a pot of tea. We had half a tin of milk left, and two heads of corn, which we saved for lunch. Dominique still had a few shreds of tobacco, just enough to roll a communal cigarette. If there were no sun that day, Jacques' photographic programme would be upset; he could not shoot what he had hoped. Our larder was empty; we could not work. We tried to accept the situation philosophically and with good humour.

I went on a tour of the camp. Mougounzi looked morose; several women kept their noses buried in their work; the men loafed idly outside their huts. Only the children were active as usual.

"Leonard—ask them what goes on today."

He had a short interview, returned with a rueful expression in his big eyes and said:

"M'sieu, because of the ants they couldn't sleep, in order to watch their families. The sky is no good, no hunting today—and tomorrow they go to shift camp to a place near Gatongo."

I sat for some time on a drum, watching them. A little boy stumbled by with a big calabash he had filled at the stream. Njaoué went back to her basket-making. Rocking her baby's cradle, she hummed a sort of lullaby version of her wonderful hunting-song—still masterly, though through half-closed lips. I was moving quietly away so as not to disturb them when a violent row broke out in Dangawé's hut.

Dangawé was angry, and talking very loudly; he was

admonishing his wife most vigorously. She never said a word. They stood before one another face to face. When Dangawé raised his hand, Ndima, before she received even the slightest blow, began to cry out so piercingly that Mougounzi intervened. He separated them, with Dangawé still protesting loudly; he whose face was normally so calm and good-humoured was now frowning, even snarling. Leonard, who had followed this domestic trouble, explained to me:

"It isn't Dangawé who's so much in the wrong. He asked his wife to cook some maize. She wouldn't do it, so he shouted. She still wouldn't do it, so he lifted his hand. But he wouldn't hit her."

"Do you suppose she'll cook his dinner now?"

"Oh, surely. Before she didn't want to, now she cries a bit, then she'll get the pot. With the women," said Leonard, tolerantly, "things are difficult."

During the row I had affected to notice nothing—except perhaps the remarkably conciliatory attitude of Mougounzi. Was that one of the chief's duties? Whether that were so or not, it worked; his authority was made quite clear.

No one else took any part in the dispute; everyone went on either working at something or continuing their reverie. Nevertheless, the argument had evidently jolted some consciences: Ndoumba and Bakaé went back to their rope-making, asking Dangawé to help, which he duly did. Only the old woman Ongonié began looking furtively around her, mumbling in her toothless mouth, with the air of one who held the whole community as witness to the disgraceful behaviour of the young married couple.

Njaoué, giving up the basket-making, began to pestle maize in her mortar. The flour, when sifted, would make soup. Beside her Ongonié was pounding manioc; she prepared it like the other Africans, to get a fine, light flour.

When the Pygmies had exhausted their roots, nuts and forest fruits they could exchange food with the other tribes. Yesterday three women had gone to Gatongo with baskets, taking with them hides and returning with grain and root-vegetables. With Leonard beside me I went to see Kolé (since I had given her a tin of jam she was no longer nervous of me) and found her making a soup, with manioc and roast groundnuts. Through Leonard, I asked what she liked best of all to eat, and the old woman—touched by this solicitude—said:

"What I like is well-cooked bananas, with fat palm-nuts. But I eat all the forest fruits."

She handed me a tin of almonds.

That we ate at all that day was thanks to Mougounzi. He came and offered us flour, and with that and the drop of milk remaining Pascal fried some fritters in palm-oil. To say that we ate them with relish would be an overstatement; however, there was nothing else. We were smoking a few cigarette-stubs, just as a porter emerged through the bush. At last, we thought, food and cigarettes . . . but no, Koundé had no such thing; he had come straight from Gandikolo and had seen nobody.

He gave me a folder, and a receipt from the Ouesso post. I had never thought, here in the heart of the forest, to get mail from France. Already Didier, Jacques and Trotty were deep in letters from their wives—the holidays had gone well, the children were healthy (or at least they were a month ago). For me, a note from a sister told of walks in the woods to find the early mushrooms, and greengages for jam. . . . I knew it well from long ago: that great copper cauldron, the smell of cooking fruit throughout all the house . . .

"Here, Noël———" Jacques interrupted my reverie, "———a letter from the S.D.A.C. Monsieur Schiltz reminds us how important it is to get something sensational. All right up to now, but what we need, clearly, is an elephant or a gorilla."

"The elephant will be difficult; Alexandre told me so. They've moved out of the area. We won't have time to chase them up. The gorillas are another matter. Hartweg told me the other day that the hunter from the mission sometimes sees one."

Trotty said, "You saw what happened when we run into an antelope. Pftt!— and they're gone, without giving us a chance to film them."

"We need to catch one alive."

"Easy enough to say."

"We haven't got either the gear, nor the licence from the Government."

"What licence?"

"Even if you catch one—you can't film it in chains, or sitting in a cage."

"Might as well go to the Zoo."

"In any case the thing's far too difficult. M. Barbereau at Ewo saw an American; he had nets made of steel cable, and that didn't prevent one of his beaters having his arm pulled clean off."

"All right—we'll see. Let's ask M. Mathieu's advice. We leave tomorrow; we'll be in Ouesso on Saturday. Okay?"

Jacques agreed. We should have to accomplish the impossible to make sure of what, in the eyes of the Producers and the Public, must be the high-point of the film.

In the early hours, just as the Babinga were making ready to go, there came a clap of thunder, and the rain began to thud down. Here came the storm that had threatened for twenty-four hours. The Pygmies would certainly not leave that day. Leonard returned to us with the news.

"They are going to stay here. You can rest. It's raining hard. I'll heat up some tea."

Three hours later it was still pouring. We sat on our beds feeling cold. Jacques decided to take some shots of the camp in the storm. Would there be enough light? Trotty, half-clad under a poncho, held the Arriflex, protected by Dominique and Jacques, who took turns carrying the battery and holding a waterproof sheet over the camera.

Regardless of the rain, the children were playing ball with a lump of raw rubber. Then, suddenly, Dangawé, Ndoumba and Mounika came out of the forest. The last two carried bunches of leaves and made a pretence of spying on their companion. Dangawé moved here and there, turning his head to left and right . . . after several minutes of this play, most expressively done, the two hunters mimed an attack on an elephant. He was wounded, he stumbled . . . the Pygmies finished him off, and everyone hurried behind the huts.

It rained, it rained. In shorts and barefoot, we mingled with the gamesters. We played a crazy game of ball; the best way to keep warm. The Pygmies, it seemed, loved it.

Chapter IX

Waiting for the Boat – Babenzélé Building – The Panther – "The Talking Machine" – Death of a Panther.

THE afternoon was ending—already it was Saturday, the 7th September—and there we were in the travellers' hut at Gatongo. The day had seen us all dispersed, singly or in little groups; now we were assembled for the evening meal under the erratic light of the storm-lanterns, their beams alive with floating insects.

Before dawn Jacques and I had left for Ouesso; in a pause between the rains we had taken leave of the Pygmies and crossed the Sangha with the Djaka ferry as the orange disc of the sun sent its glow over the muddy waters of the river. We had walked through the market to kill time until a decent hour for calling at the office of M. Mathieu; when we presented ourselves, with his unfailing courtesy he asked us to lunch. We spoke of gorillas, and he said he would write that very day to Fort Rousset, to enquire of the departmental chief whether we might have a hunting permit. The capture of gorillas was much more strictly controlled than we had imagined.

As we left, Madame Mathieu, with the sort of gentle kindness that could not be denied, loaded us with little baskets of fruit and vegetables. In any case, after our stay in the forest, few things could have given us greater pleasure. We had also bought flour, cigarettes and a pair of sandals for Motozélé. But there was still no news of the *Balin*—a little disconcerting, since we were in rather serious need now of equipment: magnesium lights and "Bengal fires" for our night photography.

Meanwhile Hartweg had been busy with anthropological measurements of the Baya of Kombo-Kombo. He had photographed them full-face and profile, both men and women, of all varieties. Then he set out on the road again, accompanied by a little black monkey which everyone had agreed to call Boubou.

Towards the end of that morning Didier, Trotty and Dominique left the camp. The previous evening we had passed the porters sent by Nief to chase up our equipment, and all that afternoon the film-men followed the Babenzélé through their great house-removal, photographing the men bearing the nets and spears, the women under vast household burdens, the children with their torches.

It was clear we were going to be here for several weeks, so on the Sunday our first care was to see to our comfort. We should certainly not be able to make any plans until the date of the next Brazzaville boat was known, and this seemed wrapped in mystery. Watched by the whole population gathered round Motozélé and Alexandre, we put up our tent, because the guest-house was certainly not nearly big enough for us all. Hartweg badly needed somewhere or other in which to set up his medical equipment; Pierre had found it necessary to build nearby a little hut that he could use as a house and a workshop. Our cook had organised an outdoor kitchen near enough to be able to shelter his pots under our neighbour's roof should it rain.

PLATE 15. Armed with their hunting-nets and their spears, a group of Babenzélé Pygmies move off for the hunt.

PLATE 16. (*above*) Njaoué, wife of the Pygmy chief, nurses little Ndoké while she weaves a large pannier. (*below*) After the share-out of meat from the hunt, Njaoué cuts up her ration to prepare supper, the only meal of the day.

Joachim had returned, apparently completely cured, but he brought with him some serious news for Hartweg. It seemed that the hunter from the Mission had been gravely hurt by a wounded gorilla; he had had his shoulders torn open and had been beaten down by blows from the creature's hand, and then left for dead on the ground. His son, who was with him, had had the presence of mind to feign the same condition, a stratagem that had allowed them to slay the animal as he was examining the bodies. The skull and bones were to be given to our friend, as soon as he could go to Ouesso to collect the skeleton.

I did not want to let the day pass without visiting the Babenzélé camp. I took with me the invaluable Alexandre, and arrived in the clearing to find Dangawé playing the drum, beating the antelope skin with a steady rhythm. It was true that the Pygmies had proved themselves superb singers, but compared with the other Africans they were only mediocre drummers. Surrounding Dangawé as he drummed lay outspread nets arranged in a curious, interesting pattern. I asked Alexandre why they were set out in this odd arabesque.

"Well, Monsieur Noël, you see—the nets are strong, but they should not be wet. You've seen how the Babinga take care before going on the hunt to see that the forest is well dried. Here they are drying off the least damp, and after a while Dangawé will mend the holes in them."

Ongonié passed us, shouldering a sheaf of sticks, and in a moment I was able to study the old woman building a new hut. The sticks, between six and eight feet long, were extremely supple, and were planted and bent in arcs, then interlaced, forming a hemispherical body, which was most carefully tested for strength.

Next afternoon, while helping us to install two big tents we had brought to the Pygmy camp, Dangawé was suddenly attacked by a little snake. Dropping from a low tree, it was about to bite him on the shoulder when, with great adroitness, he whirled about, pulling his machete and slicing it in two. There beside the brilliant halves Alexandre told us solemnly: "Listen carefully, Monsieur Noël—and you too, Monsieur Dominique. This is a very bad snake. He hangs on a branch, and he jumps. He bites you, and very soon you die. Just be careful."

Hartweg had already warned us about these little green fellows, whose venom is so efficient that it can put you out in a few hours.

Didier fixed up one tent with his bed and the recording gear; in the other he arranged the electrical stuff lent to us by M. Mathieu, the batteries and the reserve material.

There was a particularly good dinner that night: a rice pilaff with pimentos, and a most enormous fish—it had been brought by N'Goundi fishermen, hung from a staff between their shoulders, and it must have weighed thirty pounds.

While we were busy enjoying this a tremendously heavy buzzing made us look up, and, before we could escape, a vast insect, over four inches in length, dived through the lamplight into the big dish. Hartweg grabbed it instantly to preserve in a bottle, saying, "One of the aquatic hemiptera; obviously there must be marshes nearby. There are plenty of them in France, but there they are only an inch long at the most; I would never have believed Africa produced such monsters."

Towards the end of the meal we were attacked by

more and more of the creatures, obviously attracted by the light. Luckily, however, they advertised themselves by such a row that we were able to protect our mess-tins.

During the night Dominique thought he heard a noise, and got up—he found nothing, and went back to bed, but early the next morning, as we were washing, Hartweg cast a suspicious eye on the skeleton of the gorilla which was drying on the roof in the sun, and said:

"Who's stolen a humerus?"

He immediately suspected us of playing a trick on him, but when we assured him of the deep respect in which we held his collection he was more or less convinced and began to hunt about. Very soon he called out, "There's been a thief, and here are his tracks!"

Sure enough, at the bottom of the mud wall were traces of a panther, which had clearly climbed on the roof and taken a bone away. Obviously we had not passed nearly as quiet a night as we had imagined, for we next learned that Didier had nearly been bitten by a black snake, though fortunately he had managed to kill it by a blow from a stick. When it was shown to Boubou, the little ape cowered and shrieked like a terrified old woman.

Jacques, Trotty and Dominique finished filming the building of Ongonié's hut, watching the framework of sticks covered with an intricate thatch of leaves, like the scales of a huge fish, proof against almost any rain however violent. When the old woman was satisfied with her work she was prepared to give her attention to the business of filming. They photographed the whole process, from the initial leaves on ground-level through the lining of the walls to the roof.

Ndékoué, as bizarre as usual in his sky-blue hat, helped Moboma and Mougounzi to build a new hut to replace the old one which had fallen to pieces. From now on, with the heavy rains approaching, there would be more and more spare time for the Babinga men, who would be able to hunt less and less. This building was to be a sort of club-house; below the nets hanging from the roof was set up a log bench, clearly built for gossiping.

Rouget joined us with a very serious proposition: before we started to record any singing it would be necessary to make the Babinga familiar with the "talking machine". For that it would clearly be best to interview Mougounzi—or rather listen to him talk, since any sort of dialogue would be impossible. So Jacques assembled round the microphone a little group consisting of the chief, his father Télé, Mounika and Dangawé, joined in a moment by Bakembé, Ndékoué and Moboma; a collection of intensely interested people. As the machine began to turn Jacques asked Mougounzi and Télé to repeat for us the hospitable declarations they had made at our first meeting, and this they gladly did—I could recognise their sentiments by the tone of their voice, and how well had they kept their word! After this Jacques said, "Ask them now to tell us the tale of the hunt, with all the noises and shouts they usually make when they fix the nets. Try and make it just the same."

This was going to be most useful when we dubbed our film. First old Télé said a word or two; Mounika and Dangawé jumped into the nearest bushes to gather some branches, hurrying back with loud cries. The little crowd that had gathered to watch did not make enough noise to satisfy them, so Bakembé grabbed a little dog and loped back to the microphone. There was a storm of laughter and shouting as he pulled the creature's ears and made it bark.

"Cut!" said Jacques, and stopped the recording.

The Pygmies gathered round our tent-studio, and Didier played the show back to them, and thus they heard, unquestionably for the first time in their lives if not the last, the sound of their own voices. Mougounzi bent his head, put his chin in his hand in an attitude of thoughtful consideration. Télé, hearing himself talk, stamped urgently, and harangued back, while Dangawé smiled, as if he were amused. When the machine gave out the barks of the dog everyone roared with laughter. As soon as it was over Alexandre asked them:

"Are you pleased with the talking-machine?"

"Ha!"

Their approval was eager and unanimous; it seemed they were conquered by the machine; there would be no trouble with their songs. But then, as Rouget was dismantling the gear, up came the unspeakable Kolé, with the determined request that she, too, might make her record. Well, why not, we said, and for three minutes listened to a cataract of words that seemed joined into one enormous sentence. She came to an end, and retired with dignity. We at once asked Alexandre to tell us what it had all been about.

But he hesitated, and played around in embarrassment with the tail of his shirt.

"You see, Kolé is an old woman—she doesn't know you; she didn't mean anything."

That was enough to stimulate our curiosity even more.

"All right, but what did she *say*?"

133

"Very well. She is most happy to see you in the camp. She thanks you for the salt, and she would like some more tins of things to eat. And then———"

"Come on. What then?"

"Well—then she said: 'If you have come here to do things with the women, you might as well go home'."

We looked at him in astonishment, but it scarcely seemed worth an argument. Didier reassured him: "Good—you tell her if you get the chance that she can sleep easily. She has nothing to fear. We keep our own women at home."

The sky clouded over and Jacques saw despairingly that there would be no more photography that day. Hartweg went off with his tape-measures to record the dimensions of the Pygmies, who seemed quite happy to be manipulated by an anthropologist, though it required a lot of patience on both sides; if the statistics were to have any valid meaning, at least forty measurements were necessary. For the operation—obviously they thought it very important in some way—they adopted a solemn, ritual aspect.

There was a curious moment when the time came for Bakaé—the oddly shaped young man whom Hartweg, unwarned, momentarily took for a woman. After hearing Bakaé's own account, however—he was very nervous—and that of Mounika, the bosomy young man's father, he was soon able to arrive at a diagnosis.

"He is not a hermaphrodite, but a rather remarkable example of gynaecomastis. It is very unusual———"

"An example of what?"

"It's an exaggerated development of the male breast, due to a hypertrophy of the mammary glands."

And so Bakaé went through the tape-measure routine, too.

Hartweg completed his records of the Pygmies. Besides this anthropological recording he was carrying out researches on all the dead beasts brought to him, preserving bits of them in formalin for later histological examination. The day before, he had gone to Gandikolo to dissect a little chimpanzee and a peculiar fish with an elephant's head: a gnathonemus.

Logoué borrowed a gun from us to go, he said, hunting duck. He hoped he might find an antelope or a wild pig—the grim character with the sabre-tusked face often to be found wallowing in the soft ground near the marshes. He moved off in the direction of the ground flooded by the recent rise of the Sangha—walking without noise, passing almost fluidly through the lianas and entangled branches, from which the toucans fled, calling satirical cries.

He stopped and sat down, reached into his clothing and found a half-smoked cigarette, struck a match and bent to the flame—when the leaves parted five yards away, and he had just time to grab his gun, already loaded with one cartridge of small shot and one of large. The eyes of the angry panther glowed, and Logoué fired. The beast fell a couple of yards away; Logoué dealt her a heavy blow on the neck, lit his cigarette-butt and went to seek help to carry the animal.

This would be a splendid piece of standby filming while we were waiting for the gorilla-hunt. Jacques scripted the thing there and then: the Babinga would be presenting the panther to Motozélé—with a simple objective, the panther's whiskers; chopped very small and mixed with food, these were a medicine, or a spell, that is to say, they would perforate the intestines of the victim of some imaginary witch-doctor.

Immediately we built a camera-dolly—improvised one, that is, from a couple of planks on which Trotty could balance, while the apparatus was dragged over a stretch of flattened sand. But the day continued without any sun. No pictures; perhaps tomorrow. Surrounded by the entire population, Hartweg opened up the animal to eviscerate it, so that it might keep longer, carefully removed the organs for his collection and sewed up the gold-and-black skin.

Next day when Logoué came to see us his face was wildly streaked with white and black charcoal.

"For the Pomo," he said, "if you've killed a panther, the thing is to paint your face. You also wash your body and rub it with a burned stick."

"For how long?"

"For a panther—every day for a week."

"And for other animals?"

"There's also the elephant and the *bongo*, the big striped antelope. For them the same thing goes on for ten days."

Forty-eight hours later Logoué still proudly wore a face scrupulously lined and scored with ritual markings. Alexandre explained to me:

"Another thing—when a hunter is eaten by a panther, it is necessary for his relatives then to eat a panther. The men, of course, not women."

Logoué added, "Those who have the bad illness don't eat, or they will never get better."

When we were alone Alexandre said, "What's more, Monsieur Noël, when he has his paintings on he doesn't go with his wife."

"Even now?"

"Oh yes; they are in the same hut but not in the same bed. The man sleeps on the bed and the woman on the floor—or perhaps the other way round; it is the man who decides."

"And what about the man who has killed an elephant or a *bongo*?"

"That is ten days, like the painting."

The panther-sequence was a great success, with everyone taking part according to his speciality. The animal was ceremoniously drawn into the village. The camera-dolly had actually worked. Bakaé and Ndoumba were the stars, with a strong supporting cast of Babinga.

Meanwhile Didier and I were at Ouesso—for the *Balin* had at last arrived! Didier got his equipment, Jacques his lights, and the rest of us were sure of enough rice and flour, tinned fruit and jam. And, best of all, we had the precious boxes, with our only luxury: ten bottles of South African brandy, matured in the Settlement Store.

Chapter X

Back to Ouesso — The Swimming Monkeys — The Salt-Maker — Aphorisms and Maxims — Africans versus Pygmy — The Goat-Mask Dance.

HERE in Ouesso the sun was high, the palms drew around them little pools of shade, the river bank was almost deserted. Those whom I had to see would be eating, or sleeping, so I rested on a stone beside the water, where a young woman was washing her linen and humming a song. The boatmen secured the canoe and strolled over towards her—what they said I did not know but it was pleasant; she laughed softly.

Then the siren of the brickworks announced the afternoon's work, and I sought out the Greek trader, because I needed paper and tobacco. His store was full of great packs and bundles of clothes, clean but clearly second-hand, of ancient hats and rows of shoes arranged with the utmost casualness; frequently each of a pair was of a different colour, and not infrequently for the same foot. Amazed by this display I asked:

"Where on earth do you get all this stuff? There can't be a rag-merchant here?"

"But certainly not, my dear sir. You don't appreciate the situation. These are sterilised clothes, from America. I sell them—extremely cheaply—to the negroes who want to put clothes on."

"Well," I said, "I had not imagined that in this forgotten corner of the African forest there would be a market for the produce of the dustbins of New York. This is indeed progress."

The merchant merely smiled. While I paid him he handed me a newspaper—the only one printed in Brazzaville—already three weeks old.

"They're writing about your expedition, of your friends. You're famous already."

I saw the piece on the front page: "Prehistoric grottoes revealed near Brazzaville." The article pleased me because it gave me news of Erik and Francis, of Guy and of M. Bergeaud.

"A party from the Ogowe-Congo Mission," it said, "which arrived in French Equatorial Africa last July and has been in the Mayam district exploring, has made a prehistoric and artistic discovery of the first importance. . . ." and it went on to describe a series of grottoes extending for some fifteen hundred yards, hidden by the forest, with immense caverns more than thirty feet high. "And besides the scientific interest of this," the article went on, "there is no doubt that these grottoes, so near to Brazzaville, will be a considerable tourist attraction."

It made me smile a little; it seemed that our work with the Pygmies was likely to be an attraction only to ourselves.

I left the trader's shop and went along to M. Mathieu, to see if he had any good news about our gorilla-hunt. The reply from Fort Rousset was crisp: "The capture of gorillas may only be effected by special permission of the National Museum of Natural History." We could hardly write to Paris. We should have to think of something else.

M. Mathieu, ever helpful, suggested putting us in touch with Bakouélé, the hunter who kept Ouesso in fresh meat. He might agree to let the cameramen go out with him, and he *might* stumble on a gorilla.

I went to look for Bakouélé.

The market-place was empty, except for three yellow dogs arguing around an old bloodstain. Behind a brick hut was an old woman gathering rubbish. I offered her a cigarette and asked, "Bakouélé?"

Giving me a toothless smile she indicated a hut near-by, surrounded by a little garden. I knocked, and a woman appeared at the half-opened door. But she told me Bakouélé had left that morning.

"Tell him to go and see the Commandant. It's about the white men who are at Gatongo, the cinema white men."

"I shall tell him."

Before getting the canoe I went to warn M. Mathieu. He had stocked us again with fruit and vegetables, and he presented me also with Kiki, his son's monkey, and a glittering-eyed macaco ape.

"While you're waiting for the gorillas, these can be the first guests in your zoo. Come back soon."

For the first two hours neither of them gave much trouble. Kiki sat on my shoulder, content to have her skull scratched; she had the temperament of a lap-dog. The macaco was a very different character. I held him on the end of a chain that I had to shorten more and more, to prevent him darting among the legs of the boatmen to steal oranges, at the imminent risk of having them over the side.

But they paddled on. Now it was past eleven; lulled by the monotone of the creaking paddles I fought against sleep. My fingers relaxed on the chains—and, abruptly, both monkeys plunged overboard at the precise moment when a large fish contrived to leap into the canoe. One boatman tried to capture the fish, another tried to hold the canoe straight. Then the fish flicked itself back into the river, and the monkeys were hauled back dripping into the boat. The whole incident lasted about twenty seconds.

An hour later I saw the big palm, standing on the bank like a lighthouse: Gandikolo.

Rouget was still awake; he was chasing a cockerel that was making a din on the roof. I tied the monkeys to a palm trunk, while he offered me some cold meat and fruit. We spoke in whispers, not to arouse the camp. It seemed the cinema-crew had filmed the children, who had been outside the camp chasing birds with their small bows.

"What about the flares and lights?"

"After the first surprise, the Pygmies were not in the least afraid. As for me, I recorded Njaoué. That woman has a really extraordinary voice. I think it has something to do with magic. Its ritual meaning is hard to identify, but it's pretty certain that it is some sort of incantation for the hunt. The Bangombé do it too."

"When do you suggest going to them?"

"A week from now. Didier's agreeable to a shift."

I left Rouget, and again took the moonlit road to Gatongo. Kiki sat on my shoulder, the macaco trotted behind me until, after ten minutes' walking, it lost interest in moving farther. I stroked it and encouraged it; then I threatened it. The ape remained immobile. I was doubtful about striking it; the reactions of these animals are hard to foresee. I sat down beside it and lit a cigarette. The beast regarded me indifferently. I got up again and for some reason—I have no particular liking for military music—I started to whistle "Madelon". Instantly the monkey hurried ahead, gambolling along, tugging the chain. Thus we entered the sleeping village, a martial sight indeed.

Alexandre Djambabo sat before me on a little stool carved from a single piece of timber; we were in front of his house. His walls were decorated with pictures copied from a "dissionnaire"—an elephant, an antelope, a hippopotamus and a rhinoceros, interspersed with stylised trees. The rhino he had never seen, for there are none in the region. By the door he had imagined a Pygmy in pursuit of a gorilla. The silhouette of the hunter was beautifully realised, tiny beside the great ape.

Under the pent-roof of the nearest hut an old woman was preparing what seemed to be a strange dish: she poured boiling water over a cone of leaves full of ashes, and Alexandre said, "She is making salt, Monsieur Noël, with banana leaves dried for a long time and burned. The people here—the Pomo, and the N'Goundi, the Yassoua and the Bomassa, as well as the Babinga —used not to know the white man's salt. This is all right, it serves for salting the vegetables and the manioc."

Having taken down the first words of the Pomo vocabulary I was compiling on behalf of the Institute of Ethnology, I next asked Alexandre to dictate to me some of the proverbs of the Pomo. I wrote them phonetically, noting the translation word for word. "The bee took counsel from the fly" (It is no use asking advice from a lunatic). "The egg does not betray the bird" (The son is faithful to his father). "If he often returns, the antelope will eat the centipede" (Do not make the same mistake twice). For two hours I questioned him, then we went to Motozélé's home.

Motozélé's hut was set back from the rest, and surrounded by four others: one each for his three wives, one for his mother. Motozélé and his uncle, an old man still wearing the traditional woven loincloth, were eating outside with Logoué, his face still painted in its ritual stripes because of his panther. Alexandre sat down before a big bowl of rice and another in which floated portions of fish in a thick orange-coloured sauce of palm-oil. The manner of eating was to roll a small ball of rice, dip it in the sauce and swallow it, finally dipping the fingers into a bowl of water carried round by Motozélé's oldest son.

Everyone seemed to be busy in the camp. Hartweg continued his measuring of everyone he could find; he also took from each a drop-sample of blood to compare its grouping with those of the other Africans. Jacques made use of Hartweg's anthropological activities to film the short sequence of Pygmy faces which we had in mind as an opening for our film.

Jeanne, the wife of Alexandre, came in from the plantation carrying maize, which she laid out to ripen in the sun. Three Pygmy women were doing the same thing. The harvest had been good, the rains neither too spare nor too abundant. Alexandre explained to me—indicating the Pygmy women—that when the Babinga were in the base camp Motozélé required of them a certain amount of work in the fields, in return for which he gave them part of what they gathered.

"But you see, Monsieur Noël—with us it is difficult; even if you have the Babinga, you are not their master."

"How?"

"Why, you will see with these ones. With the meat,

too—when you have the Babinga they give you gazelles and you give them spears and axes and knives. And then sometimes they do not give the meat."

"Has that ever happened?"

He counted on his fingers. "Yes, four months ago, there was a big camp of a hundred and fifty Babinga here; they belonged to Mambiko, the uncle of Moto-zélé. Well, there was a lot of trouble over the meat. The uncle wanted a lot and the Babenzélé didn't want to give it. Mambiko started to take back the axes and knives, then one day the people were all gone. They are still all gone, in the forest far away, at Ikilemba."

"But who was right in this business?"

"Right?" he seemed surprised. "Mambiko gives axes to the Babinga, they give him meat—but nobody is obliged to do anything. That is how it is, if you have Babinga you are still not their master. They have not got any master."

"And if you haven't any Babinga?"

"Then, Monsieur Noël, you can trade knives for meat, and you can ask them to work in the fields and they will if they want to, but you have to give them maize and manioc the same day."

Clearly there was one sanction the Pygmies could always use against their "patron", perhaps—there is no real word to describe the Pygmy–African relationship—that of vanishing into the forest whenever they wanted to.

Next I made him tell me, word for word, the famous story of the antelope and the tortoise, "Adiemo bane Kouli". I took it down—literally, in my phonetic version of Pomo, and then in translation. It went like this:

"They argued the matter, and competed, and so the

PLATE 17. Among the Pomo Africans at Gatongo: Logoué, having killed a panther, scrupulously observes the custom of his people and paints his face with ritual signs.

PLATE 18. In the country of the Pomo Africans: the anthropologist Hartweg disembowels a panther to add the useful portions of its viscera to his collection.

tortoise took all her children and dispersed them at intervals throughout the forest. So the antelope and the tortoise began the race, and the tortoise quickly hid. The antelope galloped by, and called out. A little tortoise called a reply. The antelope called again, and another tortoise-child called a reply. And thus onwards. The antelope galloped on desperately; there was always the tortoise calling 'Come on!' And so the antelope tripped into a hole and broke her neck, saying, 'At least I am strong.' In such a fashion she died by her own strength, and the tortoise and all her family went home."

Alexandre finished, and I asked for more.

"Oh yes, Monsieur Noël, we could have the story of the Parrot and the Foolish Man, but it is very long; it is for another day. We must go and find the drummers with the Babenzélé."

"The drummers?"

"For tonight's dancing. When the Pomo dance, they borrow the Babenzélé drums. We give them rattles and bells."

"Don't the Pomo make drums?"

"Not now. Once—not so long ago—they made drums too."

The young men were now drumming, one with his hands, another with drumsticks, and the men were dancing among the circle of women. Motozélé joined us, together with Logoué, who had abandoned his shirt and shorts so that he could show his torso striped with white lines, his limbs daubed with clay; he wore the traditional Pomo dancing headgear: a tuft of parrot feathers in a semicircle. He told me:

"Now it is Djoboko and Djanga together; the men and the women dance at the same time."

"But those are Babenzélé dances!"

"Yes, they taught them to the Pomo."

In fact, the choreography that now appeared before us had nothing in common with Pygmy dancing. I greatly missed the vivacity and grace, the rhythmic sense of Mounika, the humour of Njaoué. On the other hand the Pomo drummers appeared to be more accomplished and effective. They had taken great care to tune the skins of their drums, and their unison was remarkably adaptable.

After half an hour of this, during which my eyes strayed restlessly though my ears remained attuned to the sounds, there appeared a young man in a wooden mask, the vaguely human aspects of which were surmounted by a pair of curved horns. He moved among the dancers. Alexandre murmured:

"It is Ndiba Ndiobata: the goat mask. When it is taken by someone the dance is over . . ."

And at that moment some men arrived with a litter. The drums and bells rang out; they bore away the mummer to a hut. Motozélé shook hands with us and retired, but the festivities were by no means finished. All the population, women and children too, gathered round the musicians, who abandoned their drums for rattles of basketwork—the *bwe-bwe*. A long chanting line of dancers, nodding and shaking, began to surge through the village, to the accompaniment of a random, imaginative chorus from the singers. Dominique and I joined in, and this stimulated more improvisation from the chorus. Then, under the pale light of the moon, they one by one returned to their huts; the singing died away into a murmur of pleasantries and conversation, died away further, died away as the village drifted into sleep.

146

Big things were afoot: we were going to film the Pygmy dances. The cinema boys needed our help: to hold lamps, to light the Bengal candles. Jacques assigned to everyone his part; Trotty showed us how to handle the magnesium flares.

"Always hold them at an angle, unless you want to get sparks over your hands, which hurt. When they burn out, never throw them away until you're sure they're finished——"

There was a sudden surge of cries, and we cut the details short and hurried outside. An old woman, gesticulating dramatically, appeared from the path that led to Gandikolo, and Leonard hurried to meet her. Everyone seemed to be emerging from their huts.

"The snake—the snake!"

Clearly, we thought, she had been bitten; Hartweg automatically reached for his syringe. Then Leonard called out that the old woman's cries were only of alarm; a python had been discovered asleep in the plantation, among the manioc. The only thing to do was to find it.

Three hundred yards from the village, and there it was—underneath a pile of leaves, coiled in upon itself, its head resting on the pillow of its own dully glowing scales. It was fast asleep, apparently gorged, anaesthetised by digestion. It was certainly several yards long.

The first impulse was to capture it alive—but what should we do with it on the way to Brazzaville, on the way to Paris? We were not equipped to transport it, nourish it, maintain it. That reflection condemned it to death.

The first thrust of the spear caught the snake at the base of the head, its most vulnerable part, and quite slowly it disengaged its coils, thrashing the manioc with its tail while someone else stabbed it along the line of its spine. The great serpent writhed and turned; not one of its wounds gave blood, though its backbone was clearly broken in many places. Still heaving, it allowed itself to be twined round a stake and taken back to the village—a lovely thing, with a chilly, dry, metallic hide overlaying superb muscles.

Back among the huts we measured it: five and a half yards long; thirteen inches in circumference—after the South American anacondas, these are among the world's greatest snakes. It kept a desperately obstinate grasp on the dregs of its life: it was still living at two o'clock in the afternoon, still blindly trying to strike at those who touched it, with jaws that could grasp as fiercely as those of a big dog.

Alexandre told us the Pomo used to believe that a bite from a python rendered one immune from the stings of lesser snakes; but we did not feel inclined to test the efficacy of this vaccine.

In the end, its scales dull and lifeless, Hartweg selected various anatomical specimens; the rest was carved up for distribution. Our cook assured us that the flesh was excellent. "You will see—like good fish."

And at dinner that night we tried: slices of rubber, savourless and dull: python cutlets.

That night was to be the big night; firework night, cinema night. The fire was burning; we had prepared steel holders for the magnesium flares, we had installed torches everywhere. The Pygmies were intensely excited; we had distributed leaves of tobacco and Mougounzi had been given a bag of salt. The old man Télé welcomed us with a vast enthusiasm; we suspected him of having had a palm-wine session with Ndékoué. There were many strange faces around, too—the

Babenzélé of N'Dalo, come to join the Gatongo community for the great event.

The women and children grouped themselves round the huts. For this occasion some of the girls had decorated themselves with a bouquet of leaves at the groin, as a *cache-sexe*. Dangawé and Ndoumba began to stroke the drums with their drumsticks, and the dancers lined up in two files, partners from each camp leaving the ranks to face one another. This, the "Ebandja" dance, is a sort of game based on a definite formula: when one man extends one arm it is crossed by his adversary's; when he extends his left leg his *vis-à-vis* extends his right and so on. There was a lot of feinting. The speed and style were extraordinary, and were greeted by cries of applause, and sometimes mockery.

Meanwhile we lit the photographic fireworks. Didier with the Eyemo and Trotty with the Arriflex dived among the dancers; Dominique carried the lamp, while Pierre and Nief and Rouget and I brandished torches. A wild light flooded the clearing, and vast tormented shadows leaped among the trees; from all corners scandalised and horrified birds fled into the surrounding darkness. But the Babenzélé, far from being alarmed, were consumed with delight and excitement; the lights stimulated them, and it was necessary sometimes to protect them from the fires, particularly the zealous old man Télé.

The cameras switched their attention from the dancers to the drummers, who were by now dripping with sweat under the unusual heat of all this illumination. Very soon the women and children rose and joined in, and in a little while scores of feet were throbbing against the ground in a rhythm most delicately balanced against the variants of the song. Njaoué passed in front of Trotty's camera with a sudden smile of triumph; she mocked him, imitated his attitude with the camera, peered derisively through an imaginary view-finder, all the time dancing, all the time maintaining the beat, all the time casting swift careful eyes on the little Ndoké hanging round her neck.

Then it was all over—no more lights; the equipment was packed up, the cameras emptied. Solemnly, Alexandre came with the last words from Mougounzi:

"You made the moon and the stars. The Babenzélé are pleased."

Chapter XI

The Gorilla-Hunters — The Magic of Music — How the Gorilla was taken — The End of the Hunt — "You Negroes!"

IT was nearly October; in a week our time would be up, and it would be back to Brazzaville. Hartweg and Didier would have to return to their studies; the Musée de l'Homme for the one and the Conservatoire for the other. The rains had already begun; filming was interrupted sometimes for two or three days at a time.

We had had visitors; first the missionary, a young Dutchman who came to spend three days at Gatongo. We invited him for food, but he spoke little; the Pygmies were of scant interest to him—they were not on his programme. In the morning he gathered the believers together for instruction in the catechism, and in the evening he set them on their knees for prayers. Among them was Alexandre, who with some embarrassment told me that he had been a catechist—but his zeal had flagged; the Fathers were not very generous. . . . One day, at the end of luncheon, a new family passed through the village: the wife dressed in cretonne, the children in aprons; the man carried a smart new machete of steel. "All the presents came from the Swedish Father," said Alexandre; "the woman is very nice. . . ."

Then the gorilla-hunter, Bakouélé, arrived, and Alexandre brought him to our hut. I shook his hand—it was a strong, confident hand, matching his broad shoulders. He was short and wide, with a round head on a thick neck, watchful eyes. His French was not easy, so Alexandre interpreted: "He says: he is very strong and very artful. He is going into the forest after gorillas. He says you give him a gun."

Pierre, who was nearby, reached a musket from the wall and showed Bakouélé the working of the breech. Bakouélé examined it carefully. Then he said, "Good gun. I find gorilla, him finish."

It seemed, said Alexandre, that he was leaving before sunrise next morning, perhaps for two days, or perhaps four, or perhaps three: "He doesn't know how long."

We said we would gladly wait.

Then we received another surprise visit. That morning I met Dominique on the track between the camp and Gatongo—he had been chasing more film, for the Pygmies had caught a *n'gandi* alive. He could not wait to talk but cried:

"The General's here!"

"The what?"

"The General. The big General, whom you met at Brazzaville."

And sure enough, a hundred yards on, I came face to face with General Duchaussoy, Commander of the Forces in Equatorial Africa. He had an escort of two officers and a sergeant.

"Most happy to see you here, General," I said.

"Hallo, how are you?" he replied. "I'm on my way to Ouesso—a spare day—our boat for Nola is late— had an idea of looking you up. Would like you to introduce me to your Pygmies."

"Whenever you like, sir. I'm afraid their welcome won't be very formal."

He laughed at that, but the accompanying Captain, who had been eyeing my ragged shorts, my bare torso, my bare head, my torn sandals, said with some disfavour:

"My dear Ballif. This get-up. . . . You could at least apologise."

"Never mind," said the General, "we didn't say we were coming. This is his country kit."

"Thanks, sir. You will lunch with us?"

"No, no; don't put yourselves out. We have brought some food. Perhaps we can share all round."

Half an hour later we did, and we shared some Headquarters wine too. After coffee we took the soldiers to the camp. The Pygmies by now were adjusted to almost anything—first the *soutane* of the missionary, now the stars and braid of the soldiers. Mougounzi came up to shake hands, and accept a few cigarettes; Mounika, Ndoumba and old Télé followed; for a moment there was quite a queue. But the women remained nervously under cover.

The General was clearly surprised to find these people so robust in spite of their miniature size. He was sorry not to be able to stay, but said he had to make Ouesso by nightfall. Rouget and I escorted them to Gandikolo, where the pinnace was waiting, and the General took his leave with friendly courtesy.

Hartweg had bad news. He had been called by the doctor to Ouesso: M. Mathieu had had a bad motorcar accident and was gravely hurt. Happily an aircraft, landing on the emergency strip, had been able to take him on to Brazzaville for the treatment that was impossible at Ouesso. This was sad news for us; not only had M. Mathieu been friendly to us, he had been most interested in our work and had greatly helped us.

We had filmed the dances; we now had to record the sound for them. Rouget and André established the microphone among the chorus, and called for silence throughout the camp. A baby began to cry; hurriedly the mother put it to the breast. Silence again. "Okay," said Rouget, "Let's go."

The drums began to throb. The first cries of the Ebandja, the stirring of the fight; it made three quick and lively takes. We started again—the deep voice of the men, superimposed on a quickening of the drums; the trilling of the women; we took it all on the machine and then, once again, played back for the performers. This time they showed no surprise; impassively they listened—until Didier contrived at last to capture their interest by raising and lowering the volume, causing their voices to rise and fall. This they took to be genuine magic: the power of the machine to capture their voices, and cause them to sing loudly or softly at its command.

We sat them down again and tried them with some of the discs we had brought. First we gave them a toc-cata and fugue of Bach, which began by impressing them and finally utterly disconcerted them by its endless variations on the fugal theme, by its multiplicity of organ-tones, by its combination of both at once. This sort of architectural music was not built to seduce Africans; they preferred Chopin waltzes, with their basic rhythms, their distinctive piano notes not too distantly removed from their experience with the Yas-soua xylophone.

Finally, when the Babenzélé showed no sign of going to bed, Didier announced: "Now you'll hear a really fine song," and from the machine came the voice of Ninon Vallin singing Grieg—Solveig's Song. The

Pygmies were visibly charmed by this; smiling, they listened with acute attention, unmistakably straining to grasp the nuances. Obviously the purely vocal music touched them most closely; they have no other type themselves; this patently gave them genuine pleasure.

Their enthusiasm, however, knew no bounds when, at the end of the record, Didier announced very naughtily: "That lovely lady who sang so beautifully, that is my wife." From then on, in the eyes of the camp, his prestige was unchallengeable.

Next day, while we were eating, Alexandre hurriedly arrived and announced, "Bakouélé is back! He's asleep now, but he got his gorilla. It's wicked. It's enormous."

"Where is he now?"

"The men have gone for him. This afternoon the gorilla will be in the village."

"But why didn't you tell us sooner? We could have gone with them."

"Look, Monsieur Noël, the sun is hidden. No photographing in the forest. The gorilla comes to the village—maybe it's fine tomorrow, everyone glad."

I hoped that Jacques would be. He had gone to Ouesso to prepare for our departure. We would have wished for something better, but to film living gorillas needed resources we did not have, nor did we have the permission to capture one ourselves. Our consolation was that the weather had been so bad we could not have photographed the actual capture anyway.

This is what had happened.

When he left us, Bakouélé spent the night at Gatongo, in the hut of Alexandre, and before sunrise he was on his way again, shivering in his thin cotton shirt. He slipped on his leather holster of provisions, and, his gun in his hand, made his way into the forest, over the dead waters of the marsh. He knew where the old gorilla was that he had sought before.

Throughout the day he wound in among the tangle of well-known lianas to the old gorilla's lair; it was abandoned. He followed the trail—all day he followed it, and once he came upon a pair of *boloko*, but the white men had not given him a gun to kill *boloko*, so he had not fired. When night came he threw up a rough shelter, lit a fire, ate a handful of manioc and slept.

Again he rose before the dawn, sluiced his face in the stream, swallowed some water and moved on. Midday came, and still no gorilla. He decided to return to the village. He crept unseen back into Gatongo and hid in Alexandre's house, for Alexandre would keep quiet.

The next day he moved into another part of the forest, already flooded by the heavy rains. After an hour or two Bakouélé paused to rest at the foot of a cotton-tree, and lit half a cigarette, thinking of the dress he could buy for his wife, if this white man's commission turned out well. He checked the mechanism of the gun, loaded it.

Then he heard the noise. Someone was approaching through the bushes. Bakouélé raised his gun—the leaves parted, and there was Dangawé, smiling, two yards away.

"*M'bote.*"

"*M'bote.*"

The greetings were brief, the explanations too. The Pygmy had decided to join the chase, and had brought with him one of the two ancient guns which the Babenzélé held communally. If he could help kill one of the great apes that the white men seemed to want to film,

156

he knew he would get his photograph taken too, and a present into the bargain.

In single file they moved on, careful not to crack the branches or rustle the leaves. Dangawé went ahead; he was familiar with the trails among the marshlands and the corridors between the dense underbrush. Neither spoke.

Suddenly, just as they passed the foot of a vast cotton-tree, they heard a deep growling. Without any conceivable doubt, a gorilla—and then, in a flurry of crashing branches, there it was, fifteen yards away, the great semi-human mass, matted with long, dark hair.

Bakouélé had just time to raise his gun and fire. There was a howl of anger; the gorilla was hit in the shoulder. He rose to his full height, enormous; he rubbed his wound and gritted his teeth, and then he stumbled forward, beating his huge chest with his one good arm.

Bakouélé knew that from that moment on there was no escape for the creature. He and Dangawé had time to hide behind a line of bamboos—just as another long guttural cry came from some distance off; certainly the pursuing mate of the wounded male. Without hesitation the gorilla half turned and disappeared.

Dangawé had loaded his ancient gun dating from Napoleonic times. Charging it with black powder, tamped down with the haft of his spear, he added a plug of dry fibres and finally loaded it with his spear, which he used as projectile. Bakouélé, hidden behind a great tree, waited, while the loud complaint of the wounded beast echoed in the undergrowth. Dangawé, watching, saw Bakouélé raise his hands to his mouth and himself utter a long cry of pain. He appreciated the ruse; this would bring the gorilla back to the defence of what he took to be his mate. And in a moment they heard his breathing, and saw his grotesque mask among the leaves.

Bakouélé fired. The bullet grazed the gorilla's ear; it advanced, roaring. It was only ten feet away, and Bakouélé tried to reload, but the animal was upon him. Suddenly a hollow detonation echoed through the trees, and in the cloud of smoke that followed he saw the monster stumble, a spear projecting from its stomach; Dangawé's spear.

It had been ten minutes since the first growl of the gorilla. Now he lay there, face downwards, groping at the earth with half-opened hand, grasping at handfuls of leaves. Bakouélé approached and, lifting the enormous hairy arm, helped Dangawé retrieve the spear. He was hard to move; he weighed at least four hundred pounds.

The rain began to fall.

Back in camp Trotty and Dominique, without much hope, had set up the cameras. An hour later there was a great clamour in the forest—"Hohohou, hohohou, hohohou"—and a dozen or more men appeared, towing at the end of a strong liana the great bound cadaver, which they deposited in front of our hut.

Bakouélé returned the gun; we paid him his reward, and added to it a tartan shirt of Trotty's that he had admired. "You see, Monsieur Noël?" said Alexandre, and then, turning to the villagers, "Listen: this gorilla is very big, he is dead. You see here his bullet wounds." And there they were: on the dark skin of the great barrel chest the mortal holes, from which no drop of blood flowed, somehow resembled little sea-anemones. "And there," cried Alexandre, "the great spear hole which tore his stomach; thus the gorilla died." Thus indeed, by that huge tear.

And always it rained; when could we film this?

Hartweg advised us to eviscerate the beast if we wanted to keep it. By nightfall its guts were replaced by fresh leaves; throughout the night we guarded the corpse against the prowling panthers.

Another day, and still it rained. How long should we have to wait? If we had the gorilla, we still did not have the sun.

It was certainly a remarkable animal: its measurements were formidable: for the strictest accuracy let us give precise figures: seven feet six inches in height, and nine feet in the span of its great arms. This, beside the Pygmies, was more than large, it was colossal.

But would the sun shine tomorrow?

I threw some wood on the fire. Alexandre hunched his poncho around his shoulders and yawned. To fight off sleep, I asked him to repeat the story of the Fool and the Parrot. I had heard it before, but still. . . .

"The Fool, who had never been anywhere, came to see the Parrot, and the Parrot had one foot under his wing and stood on the other. The Fool asked the Parrot: 'Friend, where has your other foot gone?' And the Parrot said: 'Friend, my children took it hunting.' So the Fool said: 'I'll wait for your children; I would like to see what game they catch.'

"Then suddenly the Parrot's family arrived, and the Parrot stood nobly on two feet. The hunters had caught much game. So the Fool said to the Parrot: 'This is too much; I go home.' And the Parrot could not dissuade him, though he tried.

"When the Fool got back to his wife he said: 'Look,

this Parrot has a new way of hunting. He cuts off his foot and sends it out on the hunt with his children. I want you to cut off *my* foot, so that *my* children can do as well.'

"So in the morning the Fool summoned all his children and said: 'Look, bring a knife and cut off my foot. Then you can take it hunting and catch as much game as the Parrot's children.' They tried; they began to cut at their father's leg, and he cried out in agony. When they stopped, he said impatiently: 'Never mind if I shout—cut away.'

"They cut off his foot. They took it out hunting. They sought everywhere, and they caught nothing. And when they got back to the village, there was the father, quite dead.

"So they buried him.

"The Fool was buried with his Folly."

The rain stopped, the breaks between the clouds grew bigger, the stars appeared. Koukilemba, Moto-zélé's brother, came to help me watch over the dead gorilla, which already was beginning to smell badly. Alexandre promised good weather for tomorrow—so I thanked him, and went to bed.

And it was good weather, too. The gorilla was laid out in front of our hut, flat on his poor dead back, with the Babenzélé gathered around him. Standing beside his gaping mouth, Dangawé recounted the vicissitudes of the hunt, and with his permanent smile he accepted our tribute: a yellow-figured loincloth, a new machete and a gourd of gunpowder.

We filmed the gorilla from all angles. Finally, Jacques asked a Pygmy to put his hand in the huge hand of the gorilla. . . . And by midday the gorilla was

PLATE 19. These Babinga Pygmies are armed with old-fashioned muskets—there are at the most three or four in each camp. Loaded with spears, which are used as projectiles, they make very dangerous weapons.

PLATE 20. Dangawé explains to the Babenzélé how he killed the gorilla.

in pieces, vanished in a big share-out. Alexandre told us that gorilla meat was quite good, for he eats only the leaves and fruits of the forest—and indeed it had the look of wild boar—but he was too far gone; I could not fancy him. The maggots were already moving over his flat face; I could not bear him now. Bakaé and Ndilo staggered away with one of the beast's arms; I dare say that part alone weighed nearly a hundred pounds.

My job was to go with Alexandre and rehearse the interview with Bakouélé that we were to record later. Motozélé came with me, and of course the "constable". The Pomo chief sat in the clearing surrounded by Babenzélé; at his feet one woman was laying a basket of corn, another a basket of manioc. Meanwhile Motozélé announced, formally: "The chief does not want the Babenzélé to live in the woods. Come and stay in our village; make yourself a solid mud house like the rest of us. Here is corn, here is manioc—clear the bush and you can have more."

He was followed by Logoué, also urging the Pygmies to abandon their gypsy life. And then, quite suddenly, without warning, the old man Télé rose and said, "We don't want to cultivate the land; that is not our work. Our god Komba sent us into the forests to hunt; that is what we do. As for cultivating and digging the ground—that is your job. That is your personal work—you Negroes."

Chapter XII

The Spirit of the Forest – "Mopéta is Displeased" –
The Unknown Dancer – Auction Sale in the Jungle –
The Wonderful Pipe – Death in the Village.

TOMORROW, said Mopéta the headman, the
great spirit of the forest called Edzingui would
come and dance in their midst. We could film and
record the ceremony—a superb opportunity.

As the first sunlight appeared in an unusually clear
sky we were on the road to Gandikolo. Jacques had
gone ahead, Trotty and Dominique had the two
cameras. I followed with Pierre, who was spending his
last hours with us; tomorrow he was to embark at
Ouesso, hopeful of reaching the Bakouélé country and
perhaps more Pygmy camps. In any case we would
meet again at Brazzaville.

When we reached the camp everyone seemed already
at work among the cameras and the sound gear; Didier
had already cut several discs of the "Yeli" song—the
strange modulated croon that we had heard from the
Babenzélé women as the men went out with the hunting-
nets. These women of this tribe performed much the
same thing. Rouget explained to me, "It's a magic
song; I've been finding out all about it. You know
these people are elephant hunters. Before the hunt the
men are not allowed intercourse with their wives, and
on the morning of their departure the women sing this
song."

162

"Do you mean to say that since you couldn't film an elephant hunt, you've got them to arrange the ceremonies which usually go before and after? This dance comes after the hunt?"

"Yes. When they kill a big male tusker they call on Edzingui, the spirit that lives in the woods, and they invite it to dance with them."

At that moment Mopéta arrived and said, "The chief says they are ready. In a little while Edzingui will come."

Didier recharged the recording machine. Nief took up his camera position; in the shade of a hut Dominique was loading a new magazine; they would certainly need it.

A slow hand-clapping began from the men, most of whom wore bands of raffia round the head. The women and children sat in rows in the shade of the huts. Then the drums began; I went near and I saw that the drumskins seemed thicker than the antelope-hide drums that the Babenzélé used, with a strange, granulated surface. These people covered their drums with the skin of an elephant's ear.

Suddenly every man in the camp ran simultaneously to the edge of the clearing. Out of the woods, revolving as he came, appeared the apparition everyone had been waiting for, hugely masked, with ribbons of raffia floating in the air—this was Edzingui. His tall hood was nearly white, the incomparable colour of new bamboo shoots, almost a pale luminous green, and on the top of it were the little hunting charms and amulets that Mopéta usually wore round his neck and wrist; the horns of a gazelle, and little tinkling bells. Very gradually the apparition approached the edge of the camp, surrounded by the singing huntsmen. The young men carried screens, clearly made for just this purpose, of some extremely light wood; doubtless there was some ritual significance in thus concealing him from the women's gaze, although this was purely symbolic, as he was visible from the waist up. He spun round faster and faster, to the beating of drums and the crashing of bells, while the hunters around him gave shrill encouraging cries. Some of these carried great branches with raffia streamers. They held these over Edzingui, appearing to caress him with them while he gradually grew taller and taller, soon towering above his attendants, then slowly diminishing to his original size. All the time, however, he remained covered from top to toe by his hood. Twice he retired out of sight in the bushes, presumably to rest, which gave us time to adjust our cameras and sound gear. Each time he reappeared the performance began again.

A few moments after his third reappearance there was an abrupt interruption. The dancers suddenly recoiled, and Edzingui himself fled to the other side of the clearing and disappeared. In a moment we saw the cause of the trouble: down the path came three white men, two of them in uniform. One of them we recognised as the assistant administrator of Djambala, who was deputising for Monsieur Mathieu at Ouesso. There was no doubt that their unexpected appearance had dismayed the whole company; it was like having the bailiffs at a birthday party. A few minutes later Amenga came up to us and said, "Gentlemen, Mopéta is displeased. The dance is over."

We tried to intercede with Mopéta, but his face was stern; he said the Bangombé were delighted to show Edzingui to us, but they disliked the presence of

PLATE 21. A woman of the Bangombé Pygmy camp drinks from a bowl fashioned by the women of Gandikolo, a village of the N'Goundi.

PLATE 22. Hartweg, his statistics and measuring completed, allows himself to be photographed among the Babenzélé women.

strangers. This was flattering to us, but very disturbing to our programme. Like turning a switch, the camp returned to normal. The Babinga went back to their work as though nothing had happened. The administrator, conscious of what must have seemed a very awkward pause, invited us to lunch at Gandikolo, where it seemed he had thoughtfully deposited a few bottles.

He had come to advise us that Monsieur Laigret, Governor of the Middle Congo, was about to pass through Ouesso. He was making an inspection of the territory, and would have to return to Franceville down the Ogowe river. Knowing that we too would have to go down the river very soon the administrator suggested that we ask if we could accompany the Governor. We agreed to make contact with him the day after tomorrow.

The next day was fine, we were happy to see, because Mopéta had promised us that the Edzingui would again dance early in the morning. Sure enough, he appeared once more out of the forest—it was like seeing the picture round again; the same music, the same drums, the same chanting and the same Edzingui symbolically surrounded by the flimsy screens. But this time, almost exactly at the point of yesterday's interruption, the dancer developed a new theme: having reached his full height, his whirling slowed, and, in the mime of a wounded animal, he collapsed slowly on the ground, and the chanting gave place to a low moan of pain.

Then it died into silence, and in his garland of ribbons Edzingui lay stretched out on the ground, immobile. The drums began again, lightly and very gradually Edzingui gathered his decorated frame together and rose to his feet, and in a moment he was once again whirling in his endless dance.

Again and yet again the slow collapse, the symbolic representation of the successful hunt. Finally, he rose no more; the dancers remained silent and immobile; the drums faded away and in a moment or two there was nothing to be heard but the rustlings of the forest and the cry of a bird, the surrounding crepitation of the insects. Thus the drama came to an end. The Edzingui rose to his feet and disappeared into the forest, followed by several men who seemed to have the task of verifying that the spirit had definitely disappeared.

The strange thing was that although the role of the Edzingui was obviously taken by one of the young men of the village, nobody professed to know who he was. It seemed, moreover, that the performance was not supposed to represent an actual elephant hunt so much as to be a collective symbol of the animal life which surrounded the Babinga in the forest and alone permitted them to survive. Anyhow, we had it all on film and on the record.

Gradually the sky clouded over; there would be no more filming today. We decided to go back to the Babenzélé camp to arrange the collection of local objects that we were to take back to the Musée de l'Homme. Nief carried with him a supply of notes in little bundles of five francs. We had also saved all our old jam tins, knowing how valuable they were to the Pygmies, but we were not going to use them as money or merchandise because that, we thought, would be to abuse their needs; we would make them a present of them. On the other hand the Pygmies had only the remotest idea of the value of money, and if we were to buy any of their domestic articles instead of exchanging them for salt, tobacco, gunpowder or cotton goods, it would be in the hope—probably illusory—of enhancing their prestige in the eyes of the neighbouring tribes. These tribes, from whom we also intended to buy certain articles, had the monopoly of trade with the Pygmies, who, for their part, had no other source of supply. To treat both people on the basis of equality would probably, we thought, have a certain psychological effect.

We sat in the centre of the camp waiting for the Pygmies to bring along the articles that they wanted to dispose of. They approached in little groups, some with their hands full, others empty, all of them anxious to take part in these exchanges, which for them seemed to have a somewhat greater importance than that of a simple deal. Mougounzi came up and offered a drum.

"How much do you want?" asked Alexandre, showing him the red notes with the effigy of the Republic.

He stretched out his hand; "*Voué!*—five," he said, with a decided air.

I handed him the five notes. He accepted the first three with a nod, but the next ones met with his disapproval. He turned them over and gave them back to me; they were dirty and crumpled. He wanted new notes. I gave them to him, and from then on there was exactly the same reaction from all the Pygmies. Dangawé and Ndoumba laid before us a heavy hunting-net; they said they would have plenty of time to make another before the next dry season. Bakaé and Moboma allowed themselves to be separated from their spears, old Télé from his axe, and so on until all the men had passed by. The women followed; Ongonié presented us with a pot, and Njaoué gave me a little basket. They allowed us also to take away a cooking-pot, a pestle and mortar, some calabashes and some of the large flat boards of bark which the cooks used to crush nuts. Old Kolé ended the procession, offering us a spoon made of wood.

"What do you want for that?"

The old woman stuck out her thumb. I handed over a crisp new note, but she would not go away, she continued to stand in front of us and began to whine, her eyes fixed on the jam tins behind us. It seemed a pity not to satisfy her.

"Come on, don't cry, here are three big ones if it will make you happy."

She hurried away, hugging them to her breast; in a moment she was surrounded by all the other women, who immediately began to line up before us again. In no time at all our basket was empty.

I sent Leonard to ask old Télé if there was any chance of our getting hold of the big pipe, the one which the Pygmies passed from mouth to mouth when they joined together after the hunt or on the long days when the rains kept them in the camp, gossiping round the fire. It was a very remarkable pipe; Alexandre had already told me its history. It was made of a huge ox's horn, and had been brought to the village many years ago from the interior by Logoué, who had been working at the time on the Congo railway. The point of the horn had an extension of wood and carried a bowl of beaten iron. Taba, the smith, had constructed this curious affair, which was now polished by daily use to a brilliant gloss. The whole arrangement must have been nearly two feet long. I had often admired it when the Pygmies were using it ceremonially. Like the other Africans, they contented themselves with pressing their lips against the base of the horn, drawing in one large lungful of smoke, and at once passing it to their neighbour.

I tried to persuade the old man that our interest in the pipe lay in its curiosity and not in its usefulness, but he refused to hear of parting with it. Alexandre explained to me:

"You see, Monsieur Noël, you can't ask them for the big pipe, it is a souvenir of the old chief, the father of Motozélé. He gave it as a present to Télé some years before he died. In those days Télé was the chief of the Babenzélé, but now he is too old. He is still the spokesman, but it is Mougounzi who is in charge."

It seemed ungracious to insist. We went back to Gatongo with our collection, cleaned it up, powdered it with D.D.T. and packed it away in our provision boxes.

It was now the turn of the Pomo, the other tribesmen, to make their offering. They came with a hunting-net, with a spear, another man brought a bow, a leather quiver and some arrows. These arrows—with poisoned tips—were used to kill birds and monkeys. One man gave me a sort of large nut pierced with a hole and without its kernel; it made a whistle which he said enabled him to attract monkeys. Another came forward with a band of fur in his hand. It was about thirty inches long and six inches across, and its hair was dark and dense. I didn't like to refuse it, but I had no idea what it was for. I was told, "It is the skin of the otter, the river beast which is so good to eat. If you carry this fur round your arm or round your stomach, you have the strongest possible charm; you can chase the elephant with impunity." So I gave back the talisman to

169

its owner; we were not going chasing elephants and it might be useful for those who were.

An old man limped forward, gross with elephantiasis. He laid before us a wooden helmet, saying simply, "This is for war, but the wars are over, the white man came and the Pomo are quiet again," and dragged himself off. Then the women came, in a flood. We were very soon submerged under a load of cooking-pots and implements. They presented us with baskets, with sieves and with the little woven mats which they used as plates when eating their manioc and their cooked bananas. Meat is always served on leaves. They also brought carrying-baskets of different sizes for grown women and for children. They were strictly utilitarian, less decorated than those of the Pygmies.

My job was not only to make an inventory of everything that came our way but also to take down the relevant information about each article: its name, who had made it and its exact purpose. This was made a little easier for me by the fact that I had been watching them all the time that I had been staying in the village. Most of the Pomo cooking-pots had no decoration at all apart from a few geometrical figures around them; otherwise they were the same as those of the Babenzélé, although they were better made and their size was of course adapted to that of their users. In the end the choice became so large that we had to limit our collection, trying at the same time to divide our purchases equally.

"Governor Laigret is quite willing to take us to Franceville, and Dominique will come with us," announced Jacques and Trotty, just back from Ouesso.

"And when does he leave?"

"Three o'clock in the morning. He expects us the

night before; we shall leave you the day after tomorrow."

This time it really was good-bye, and there was nothing to do but prepare for it. We should have liked to have stayed longer in the village, but we had to keep to our programme, and our work here was over. What lay ahead was the rapids of the Ogowe, and possibly the opportunity of meeting more Pygmies. I slept well, thinking of the last stage of our journey.

The cold moon glanced across the foot of my bed. Half asleep though I was, a vague noise penetrated my conciousness. It seemed to me that sometimes this sound grew louder and faded and began again; I became intrigued in spite of myself, and tried to define what sort of noise this was. It was impossible to place either its source or indeed its nature. By and by Dominique beside me awoke too.

"Can you hear it?"

"Yes. It seems to come from the village." A moment later, "No, it comes from the forest, listen."

We listened together. This curious muffled noise continued to rise and fall and pause and begin again. It was obviously impossible to try to analyse it while lying in the tent. We dragged on our trousers and went out. It seemed as though the sound had got stifled in the enormous forest all around us.

With a vague feeling of insecurity we walked through the main avenue of the village. The sounds continued, and more and more it seemed as though they were human cries. We decided to risk embarrassment and knock on the door of Alexandre's hut. We called his name.

"Hullo," came a sleepy voice.

"It is us, Dominique and Noël. What is going on?"

"I don't know, I am asleep."

"All this noise that has been going on for the past hour—is it going to last much longer?"

"But, yes, Monsieur Noël, all the night."

"Very well," said Dominique, "tell us what it is all about."

"Why, it's death, Monsieur Noël. The aunt of Logoué, she has passed on."

An odd phrase, I thought, but we continued to talk through the door.

"Where is she?"

"In her hut, all her family and the old women are mourning her mortal remains."

This grew better and better. I remembered that Alexandre had learnt his French as a catechist in the mission; the pious platitudes of the grave came easily to his lips.

As we went back to our hut the mournful murmur continued to rise and fall, strange and somehow unreal.

Next morning the entire population of the village joined the long *cortège*. The cemetery was no more than a piece of the bush cleared outside the village, with no markings to show where the graves lay. In former times the dead had been buried anywhere in the forest that seemed convenient. The body is wrapped in straw mats —the number depending upon the fortunes of the defunct—and then laid in a shallow grave, and earth piled on it by the nearest members of the family. In this instance, the deceased being a widow and childless, the old woman's neighbours assisted in the task. The lamentations of the previous night had been succeeded by a profound calm.

On the way back to the village, the ceremony accomplished, I interrogated Mougounzi on the way in which

PLATE 23. Every Pygmy child—whether of the Bangombé or the Babenzélé—must learn how to drum.

PLATE 24. An instrument apparently exclusive to the Pygmies is this wooden drum.

the Babenzélé buried their dead. His reply was laconic, "They dig a hole in the middle of the camp among all the huts. They put it in, and then they leave the village."

Neither the Pomo nor the Babenzélé believed in tombs or memorials; they accepted death much as they accepted life, with a tranquillity that seemed somehow dignified and enviable.

Chapter XIII

Learning the Language – Songs on a Sandzi *– "White Men, White Men!" – Another Encampment – Down the River.*

THE sun hung in a crystal sky. If it had not been for the tremendous humidity, the climate would have resembled a pleasant May day in our own country. The film men took advantage of this our last day to make a sort of reconstruction of the gorilla-hunt sequence. Dangawé marched through the trees firing his old gun, which looked like nothing so much as an interesting relic from an antique shop but which in his hands, loaded with a spear, was a very dangerous instrument.

Forty-eight hours later we were in Ouesso. The entire population seemed to be gathered to salute the colours in the presence of the Governor. Among the crowd I noticed a most obvious and elegant personage, of the blackest hue, wearing a tweed coat, grey flannel trousers and what can only be described as a globe-trotter's hat. It seemed he was a son of the Reformed Church, who had just returned from Sweden with a motor bicycle and his luggage full of serious music. He played the harmonium in the church. I had a great ambition to stop and discuss matters with him, but already we were involved in the serious performance of the day. Very soon, glasses of champagne in our hands, we were listening to the Governor's enquiries about our journey and our work among the Pygmies.

The departure of the *Lorraine* had been put forward. She had slipped away under our noses yesterday morning, and there was no other boat for a month. I did not hide my disappointment from Monsieur Thébault, who suggested that I present my problem to two inspectors of the company who were about to return to Brazzaville in a little steamboat called the *Victor Augagneur* which would leave on the 7th October. We explained our predicament to them.

"Come by all means if you like—it's at your own risk. You will have to camp out on the deck. Have you got a cook?"

"Yes. We have to take him back to his country."

"Right. We go on board Sunday. We expect to leave at six-thirty on Monday morning."

I went back to Gandikolo to collect Didier, Rouget and Nief, who had left the Bangombé camp and hoped to record the Yassoua. Nganda, the chief of the N'Dalo, had kept his promise. He had sent his three xylophones and his best instrumentalists, and before leaving I waited awhile to listen to this excellent orchestra. Two teams of musicians played alternately; they were semi-professionals moving from feast to feast among the surrounding villages.

The last two days passed with enormous speed in long conversations conducted with the help of Alexandre. Through them I tried to finish establishing a typical vocabulary of the Pomo and the Lingala. This last idiom, which is spoken on the Likouala and around Mossaka, has gradually spread towards the north along the borders of the Sangha as far as Nola, and towards the south following the Congo as far as Brazzaville; thus it becomes a kind of *lingua franca* in all these regions. Here it was used simultaneously by

175

the Pomo and the Babenzélé; nobody here understood the language of their neighbours.

From a preliminary examination of his files Hartweg was able to conclude that the Babenzélé did not share a common blood-group with the Africans, of whom the majority are in group A or group O. On the contrary, the incidence of group B—the most important group among the yellow races—is remarkable among the Pygmies. This seemed to suggest a factor that had not hitherto been studied among the Babinga.

We started the camping equipment and the collections on the road to Gandikolo, we ourselves accompanying the last convoy. It had rained all the day and all the night, and we travelled through a tornado. Enormous drops of water splashed on the track; just in front of me Hartweg was jumping from pool to pool trying to shelter the little monkey Kiki under his poncho. I had charge of the macaco, which was soaking wet and trotted along with its head bent. On my thumb I carried a little Gabon parrot delightfully coloured in grey and red. It had been a present from a Yassoua hunter who had come with the musicians. It had no conversation to speak of, but it whistled, played the castanets and rattled with manifest talent.

Rouget had spent these two days seeking out a singer who was well known in all the district—Mandélé-Ndoumbé—a Gandikolo man and the celebrity of his village; our difficulties in tracing him had been due to the fact that he was always on the move, invited from ceremony to ceremony. Caught between two engagements, he had agreed to return for a few hours just before our departure. Rouget was well rewarded. His tenor voice was beautifully controlled, and moreover he had an astonishing mastery of breathing, accompanying himself on a *sandzi*—a little trapezoid box provided with a sequence of metallic tongues vibrated by the thumbs. His art, which was pure improvisation, was an audible denial of the old theory that African music is nothing but endless repetition. It is only the chorus, comparable to that of the ancient tragedy, which follows the immutable form. Mandélé-Ndoumbé always sang on a couch. At his left a man beat two rods together; at his right sat a blind man, completely silent, with an immobile face of such serene gravity that I could not take my eyes from it. Only when the voice reached the maximum of its powers did the blind man's face quiver slightly.

This music, "Dongho Sô", is sung for the dance of the Sons of Sô, a mythical animal which is supposed to live in the forest and is the patron of a local secret society. This creature is said to appear during the initiation of the young men, who when they enter this society are called the sons of Sô. They can be identified by a scar in the form of the letter W (supposed to be the toothmarks of the Sô) which they carry on their right shoulder. The society is open only to men, and no women are permitted even to view its ceremonies, on pain of death.

Towards the west, on the other side of the river, the sky was striped with long, grey clouds. At six o'clock in the morning, in a light somehow reminiscent of a winter evening, we embarked on the pinnace, after having loaded our apparatus, our canteens and our boxes. It was an emotional moment for the village of Gandikolo, and the old man Akili darted from one to the other of us to shake our hands in his, while Zabou ran among our legs tugging at our trousers and calling out: "White men, white men!" as though he would have us stay.

Alexandre arrived with Motozélé, in the company of Mougounzi, old Télé, Dangawé, Mounika and the rest. Mopéta and his men had been helping to carry our luggage. For all that, we had seen very little of the Pygmies during the day. None of the women or the children from the camp had come. We were not too anxious to prolong the farewell, and after a last distribution of gunpowder and caps we started down the river.

As we left, a sudden squall of rain drove all our friends back towards the village and caused us to hide underneath the roof of the boat. As we moved away, I saw old Télé waving us a final salute before disappearing in his turn. We sat silently among our valises and our cases, not knowing when we would come back, or if we would come back. In the last few short weeks we had come to love these men. Somehow I had not expected the sharpness of this parting.

So we came to Ouesso. In the afternoon the rain stopped and we were able to load our boxes into the lighter for the steamboat. We put up our beds on the deck, which was happily protected by a long roof. Then the rain began again, fine and cold, and for once we found ourselves with nothing to do. I wrote up my diary by the light of a candle.

Dawn found us leaning along the bulwarks while two sailors raised the anchors. The sirens gave three quick hoots followed by a long and sombre blast. The settlement slipped slowly behind us, and we began to move between the dense green walls which were to imprison us until nightfall. Here and there a yellow blossom or the spangles of a flowering tree punctuated the

178

monotony of the forest. I went to find out if the cook, Joachim, and Leonard had everything they needed to prepare our meals. Leonard was full of excitement at beginning what he considered an enormous voyage—I had come to admire this African pleasure in vagabondage, in travelling for the sake of moving without particularly caring where they went. We passed a canoe manned by three fishermen, with the harpooner staring into the depths of the current. I tried to fish too, and threw a line from the boat. Ten times, patiently, I pulled up my big hook, baited with a lump of meat. "You'll finish by catching a crocodile," said Didier, completing my discouragement.

Just before evening a storm obscured the sky with enormous violet clouds, and the rain began to fall with such force and density that it blanketed the riverside and seemed somehow to confuse itself with the waters of the river. The little steamboat advanced, panting, in a universe of water. But it did not interfere with our progress and very soon we saw fires burning on the banks, revealing a landing, where we tied up. The engine stopped, the cables went out and we were at the port of Pikounda.

Happily—since we were to pass two days here—it was a place of great charm. Under a group of enormous oil palms stood the house of the company agent, Monsieur Roy. It was Monsieur Roy who told us of a Pygmy encampment not far away from Matélé. He suggested that he take us there, and we were delighted to accept, curious to make some comparison with other Pygmies. As we were going there by lorry over an excellent track, I noticed on each side of the road a number of curious bell-like structures, some of them about a yard high, some of them more, and all of them covered with great leaves.

"Why are all these huts of different sizes?" I asked.

The driver undeceived me, laughing. "But no, those are ant-hills. We, the Bonguili, like to eat the little creatures inside, which are very fat, and what we do is, we cover the ant-hill with big, dry leaves and dig a hole all round. Under the leaves we light a fire of damp wood. The smoke drives the ants out, they fall into the hole and so you can collect them."

From Matélé we went on foot towards the camp, which was located under the trees two hundred yards from the village. The hemispherical huts were identical with those of the Babenzélé and similarly placed around a clearing. The villagers, thirty or forty of them, welcomed us without showing the least fear; they had already received visits from Europeans who had been passing along the trail. On the whole, their physical characteristics were similar to those of the Babinga, though some of them, more particularly the women, were of a most exceptional thinness. Furthermore, I seemed to remark on their faces an expression of singular stupidity, which may well have been due to our unexpected appearance. We had time to examine their cooking utensils, their calabashes and their mortars, which were made for them by the Bonguili women. The difference was in their big baskets, which, although similarly ornamented, were rectangular in shape and made of a thicker variety of rush. The spears leaning against the huts were longer than those of the Babenzélé, some of them almost three yards in length. They did not seem either to make or to use nets. Rouget asked them to show him their drums, but they had none.

PLATE 25. At the end of the ceremony Edzingui, phantom of the forest, falls once more to the ground, before seeking sanctuary among the trees.

PLATE 26. (*above*) The old man Télé and his friends smoke a pipe together under the common roof. (*below*) A Pygmy hunts a gorilla: drawing by Alexandre on the walls of his hut at Gatongo, the village of the Pomo Africans.

While we were making the usual distribution of tobacco before leaving, I noticed a man sitting before a hut who held in his hands the same two wooden sticks of which Alexandre had spoken to me when we were in the forest, and which the Babinga used for making fire. I asked our interpreter whether the Balouma still continued to use them, and when he replied affirmatively we told him how much we would like to film this procedure. Didier had his sixteen-millimetre camera with him, but since he needed more light we took the Pygmy outside the camp. He knelt down holding one of the sticks between the first and second toes of one foot, and with a rapid and continuous gesture he turned the other stick between the palms of his hands. In the cup at the end of the stick lying on the ground the friction produced an extremely fine powder from which a drift of smoke began to escape. At once he stopped. The sawdust began to smoulder like touchwood. With an adroit and practised gesture he gathered these tiny embers into a leaf and, with a gentle breath, encouraged them into flame.

The *Victor Augagneur* left Pikounda under a moon that silvered the darkness of the river. Only the quiet thudding of the engines interrupted the silence of the night, as we crawled down between the two interminable vegetable walls. To feel the impact of the almost terrible grandeur of the endless equatorial forest it is necessary to contemplate it not just for hours but for tens of hours and for days and for nights as well, preferably from the deck of an ancient boat, that seems itself almost to belong to the antiquity of the forest. In the days when we were marching under the high branches of the trees or forcing our way through the densest of undergrowth, our horizons were limited by the most immediate things. Although the forest was familiar to us, it was hard to be impressed by its immensity, its endlessness and its power. Now, with the green tangle relentlessly hemming us in, it seemed as though there were nothing in the world but forest.

The day followed the night, the sun followed the moon, and the little steamboat crawled along like an insect lost in the maze of an enormous swamp. As we approached the confluence with the Sangha the landscape almost imperceptibly began to change. Up to now we had wandered through the meanderings of a river dotted with islets, with enormous interlaced trees, dense with a network of creepers; now we were surrounded by a low, swampy vegetation of reed and papyrus. Alone, under the sombre stormy sky, the slender outlines of palm-trees were silhouetted against the black sky.

We passed the Equator.

Once again the inevitable storm broke, and the enormous drops of rain falling on the roof were like the sound of a tambourine. As the damp, wet hours passed, almost imperceptibly the temperature began to drop. In the growing cold it seemed pleasant to go downstairs and watch the stokers for ever feeding the furnaces with vast logs of wood. Every time the doors opened, the long, flaming tongues leapt out and licked their glistening bodies with a ruddy glow. The roar of the fires mingled with the dull mutter of the thunder outside and the rattle of the rain on the deck; sometimes the tall iron chimney exploded into the air a volley of sparks, which were caught by the wind and sent whirling into the green darkness all around.

Another day came with nothing to look at but sudden

flights of enormous storks or sometimes the passage of a troop of buffaloes; there seemed to be no other life besides themselves and us. We stopped at Boléko before a rich coffee plantation, where we unloaded some cargo: that had been the reason for our detour. A few hours later there was another stop. We paused for refuelling while the population of a riverside village filled our hold with more wood.

We reached the Congo at last. It seemed like another sea. At this point it was more than seven miles across, and on the far side the forest was no more than a dark, thin line separating the water from the sky. And then at the junction with the Likouala we came to Mossaka, which is known as the Venice of the Congo.

We took on tubs of palm-oil and baskets of dried fish. The captain asked us to put our baggage in the hold and fold up our beds on the deck—and next day, when the loading was done, we congratulated ourselves at having put our affairs in order, because both the lighter and the boat were suddenly invaded by fantastic hordes of the most extraordinary caterpillars, somehow combining the characteristics of the louse and the earwig. We found them in our clothes and in our beds, on the decks and on the chairs. There was nothing to be done about them. It seemed that the insects had escaped from the baskets of fish destined for the native quarters of Brazzaville; for a day and a half they took control of the ship. No one ever explained why, but two days later they had completely disappeared.

And then at last we were among the long, flat islands, the sandbanks and the scattered islands of the Congo itself. At seven o'clock in the morning we came to Kounda, a little village, almost completely flooded. All the houses and the tracks that led to them were built on piles at least a yard high. It needed a few feet more of water to submerge them entirely. I bought a little black tortoise there, with the wrinkled skin of an old woman. I wanted to make her the mascot of the expedition, but as soon as she reached the deck she took advantage of a moment's inattention to escape, and in spite of all our efforts we could not find her. It was practically impossible for her to have fallen into the water because a bulwark surrounded the entire ship. Later that same day I heard a sudden squalling from my little parrot. I paid no attention: she was fond of sitting on the roof, and would always come down if I stretched out my hand with a few peanuts. At a second cry, however, I looked around, and there was the parrot in the middle of the river. She had certainly only just fallen overboard because she was not more than twenty yards away from the boat, although the distance was increasing every moment. There was no way of saving her. She beat her wings, a tiny handful of living feathers on the enormous flat expanse of the river. I gave her up for lost—and then I saw a new agitation among those red plumes, and the parrot succeeded in climbing aboard a little raft of reeds that the current was carrying by. No doubt it saved her life. I waved her *bon voyage*.

More and more boats passed us by, flying the Belgian or the Congolese flag. There were tugs dragging behind them long strings of barges, proof of the richness of this colony: we passed immense rafts of floating wood on which men had constructed huts, with chimneys smoking as though they had been there for years. I amused myself by diving from the prow of our steamship, pulling myself up a little later on one of the two canoes which we trailed behind us like dinghies.

The water was tepid and the sun dried me in a matter of moments.

Our last day on the river was spent steaming between steep escarpments, and when we woke next morning we saw before us the Island of Bamou, the landscape pale in the early light. Slowly and with determination the *Victor Augagneur* came into Stanley Pool; this was nearly journey's end; we offered a bottle of brandy to the Captain, and there was the port of Brazzaville.

Chapter XIV

*Back to Brazzaville — Making a Bridge — A Meal and
a Story — With the Seven Canoes — The Buffalo Hunt —
"A Woman is a Calabash" — The Town of Brazza.*

IT was necessary to stay eight days in Brazzaville.
There was no aircraft for Paris, no lorry for Franceville; there was, however, a warm welcome from the
Governor-General. We ourselves gave a party for the
personalities of Brazzaville and Leopoldville, enter-
taining them with an account of our work among the
Pygmies; the records—the voice of Njaoué, the songs
of Yeli and Edzingui—made a huge sensation. We
were also asked to give several broadcasts over Radio
Brazzaville.

We left on Tuesday, 22nd October. Samba drove
the truck. Leonard decided to come with us as far as
Okoyo, where he would wait for a chance of getting
back to Ouesso. I left Hartweg and Nief with the
assurance that they would take a military aircraft towards the end of the week; Didier would come with us
as far as Franceville and show Dominique how to work
his equipment. And then by way of Libreville and
Lagos he would find an Air France machine to take
him back to Paris.

All along the plantations which bordered the track
to Franceville the women were already at work, sometimes with a baby on their back, its head bobbing to
the movements of its mother. After passing Okoyo, we

had scarcely travelled fifteen miles when we had to stop at the banks of a river; the bridge was under repair. The river was no more than fifteen yards across, but it was obviously very deep. They said it would take at least five days to get across, and there was no other road. We decided to try to make a temporary bridge that might support the weight of our truck. The engineer of the bridge department, who was near by, a young man from Pointe Noire, thought it might be possible to construct on the existing piers of the bridge a wooden platform made of logs and heavy branches. His workmen were there, and he got them busy with an ingenious derrick of his own construction, while we went back down the road to wait.

In the afternoon, when we returned, we found the bridge made. Very slowly, very carefully, Didier took the heavy truck over it. One of the branches cracked. Didier didn't hear it and continued his slow progress, guided by Samba on the opposite bank. The truck was two-thirds across when the bridge lurched quietly to the right. Everybody held their breath. We had unloaded most of our gear in order to make the truck as light as possible, but I was terrified for Didier; if they should overbalance how would one ever get him out of the truck?—which was, of course, the reason why he had taken the place of Samba in the driving-seat. The lorry got to within one yard of the bank; the makeshift bridge tottered but did not fall. The front wheels reached the bank. The back wheels reached the bank. We all drew breath again. There was nothing left to do but to shake hands all round and reward the crew that had created this remarkable piece of basketwork, which had managed to carry our three tons in safety.

A little farther up the track a light lorry stopped us

187

with a letter from Jacques. The boatmen had arrived; they were impatiently waiting for us.

The country through which we were passing grew hilly, but the twisting road was in first-class condition. We crossed a reinforced concrete bridge over a torrent; Franceville could not be far away. The mists dispersed, and there in the valley of the Passa lay the settlement founded in 1880 by Savorgnan de Brazza in a country which reminded him of France. Five minutes later we were in the guest-house hut, and in its dark corners I recognised our bags and cases, the cameras and the boxes of film.

"Jacques?"

No answer. We called again, and then from a neighbouring hut out ran Jacques, Trotty and Dominique.

"At last, there you are."

They introduced us to Madame Charney and her husband, the Assistant Administrator, whose guests we were. All through dinner we chatted eagerly.

"What was the Congo like?"

"Magnificent. Ballif fished for crocodiles."

"And we were nearly devoured by caterpillars that came in sacks of dried fish. But what have you done?"

"Hunted buffaloes and gorillas. Once Trotty would have been torn to bits if Dominique had not fired in time. It happened in the Zanaga region—one fine morning all the men of the village set out with us into the forest. With the help of their nets they managed to encircle a gorilla just as big as that one at Gatongo."

"And you filmed him alive?"

Unhappily not, it seemed. Trotty had had the camera, Jacques followed him close behind carrying the accumulators, and Dominique was in front with his musket ready to fire. "We were inside the nets trying

PLATE 27. Among the Badouma Africans of Lastoursville: another dance. This one centres on two masked figures entirely clad in fibres and raffia. The feathered being, symbol of virility, face to face with the feminine character whose back is to the camera.

PLATE 28. A mask of the Badouma: a female symbol, carved to hide the face of a man, combines an expression of celestial serenity with one of glorious mortal sensuality.

to approach the gorilla, which was trying to get out. He charged, and in a few seconds he was upon us. Dominique fired, the gorilla was hit in the heart."

"Just as well. I would sooner have you alive than the gorilla."

And so the meal passed with the reminiscences and gossip of those who had worked hard and worked well.

We accompanied Didier to the banks of the Passa; one of the big canoes which was going to carry us took him away in a light mist. There was a certain sadness in seeing him go; the disappearance of one of our companions seemed to presage our own return to France.

It began to rain. Trotty went over his equipment. Dominique and Rouget recorded the local school-children, who made an excellent choir. Among their repertoire of songs was one which recalled the days of de Brazza himself:

"En marchant vers l'inconnu,
Toujours seul et mal vêtu
U . . . U . . . U . . . que Brazza a bien su,
Que Brazza a bien su."

We ourselves were now in a hurry to embark, to do in reverse five hundred miles of the road followed by Brazza in the course of his explorations. From 1875–1878 and then again from 1879–1882 he established the French position on the right bank of the Congo.

The seven canoes were lined up along the bank, already loaded with our bags and gear and carefully covered with matting. One last handshake all round and our flotilla moved off in a five-hundred-yard echelon. Jacques and Trotty went ahead in the canoe of Patricio Mabouédi, the leader of the convoy. Rouget,

Dominique and I took a canoe each. Two other boat-men transported Thomas, our new cook, and his two sisters, who would never leave him, so he said. The last canoe was heavily loaded with some of our most precious luggage.

These canoes were some ten yards long and never more than three feet in the beam at their widest. They were like all the equatorial *pirogues*, hewn out of the solid trunk of an enormous tree. Flat-bottomed, with never more than a few inches of free-board and draught, they seemed to skim over the water. Each canoe had a crew of twelve to sixteen men, who sat in pairs on a plank, a boy perched behind with a steering paddle. Two men always stood in front to act as pilots. Behind them the passenger did the best he could for himself among the piles of luggage. The boats were decorated with little flags of white cloth, which flapped in the wind as we proceeded down the river.

"It is just to make a good show," called my head canoeist, Jean-Baptiste, over his shoulder. Round his neck he wore an enormous aluminium medal, and the tails of his shirt flapped against my face.

The boatmen paddled steadily though not very fast, and the bells hanging at the prow of each canoe clanged gently to the rhythm of their arms. Some of the bells were locally made out of beaten iron, others, clearly European, were made of bronze; they clanged gently in a sort of erratic chorus from canoe to canoe. "They help us on our way," said Patricio.

Again the heavy drops of rain spat on the surface of the river, and a cold wind sprang up. We put ashore at the village just as the deluge broke. We only had time to unload the equipment, and cover the more delicate machinery and fling ourselves into a hut before the sky opened and the downpour descended upon us.

We ate in the dusk with Patricio sitting at the door playing a gentle melody on his *sandzi*. He was enough of a virtuoso to make it well worth listening to him; with the rough metallic tongues of his instrument he made something very near to music.

In the first glimmerings of dawn I went out with Jacques and a hunter. We crossed a broad prairie extending behind the huts to the limits of the forest, and it was not long before we came upon three buffaloes with a calf, about two hundred yards from us. Jacques and the hunter loaded their guns and took off the safety catches. As we came out of the undergrowth the buffaloes moved off gently in the direction of the marsh. We followed them to within fifty yards when suddenly one of them lifted its head, seemed to scent the wind and abruptly led them all off at a gallop.

The huntsman soon found their traces in the damp ground. We stumbled through a marsh until we came upon them again, grazing peaceably on the soft grass. At twenty yards Jacques and the hunter each chose his victim, aimed and fired. Once again they fled, but one of them was certainly wounded; he had left bloodstains on the grass.

But Jacques wanted to go back for some more photography, and left me his gun. In silence, without any success, we continued to plod over the savannah. Then, just as I too had decided to abandon the party and go home, all of a sudden there was the buffalo ten paces away, completely immobile. I no sooner saw the one than I saw another behind him. I was completely taken aback, my gun in my hands, unable to make any useful gesture. It was a superb animal; he stared at me with his great placid eyes and then slowly walked away, a vast red bull on a broad green field.

When I got back to Mounzei the inhabitants were in transports of joy. Dominique had just made some records and played them back; the villagers were overcome with astonished delight—so much so that they had begun to dance to their own singing. The first thing they asked me was that we should send them "a machine of the same quality for making music."

About midday the hunter came back; he had killed a buffalo. When it was brought in we distributed fresh meat to all the boatmen, together with *chicons* of manioc. These are rolls of grey flour-paste in a damp leaf, which preserves them for many days.

The next day, All Saints Day, we had to shoot the rapids. With the ciné-camera at the head, our canoe squadron gingerly approached. The boatmen changed their paddles for long poles, which would allow them to steer the craft between the whirlpools and half-concealed rocks. Patricio had chosen a channel where the canoes would have to go one after the other. The more adventurous boatmen did not hesitate to jump chest-deep into the water, wrestling with the canoes among the rocks, fighting against the violent currents down towards the quieter water. At last it was all over, the manœuvre was completed; Trotty had managed to film several feet of the adventure, and the sun had come out. We lunched quickly on the fine sand, and bathed. Jean-Baptiste advised us not to go out too far, the whirlpools were dangerous and, said he, "The crocodile can easily take off your leg."

After the Moulidi rapids, Boukoussou was the end of our first stage. All the population, warned by the ante-

PLATE 29. One of the Badouma of Lastoursville: a member of the audience, her face ornamented with ritual paintings, about to reveal herself as a startling singer.

PLATE 30. At Lastoursville, among the Badouma Africans: a dancer on his points, legs and arms outstretched, stands with every muscle vibrating with an ecstasy of movement.

lope-horn trumpets, were assembled to give us a welcome, singing and clapping their hands. By now the boatmen were in their home country; each of them rushed to choose before darkness not only the best hut but perhaps a pretty companion to put in it, for according to the saying of the river people: "A woman is a calabash into which you may dip, but which you mustn't take away."

A man went from group to group playing a curious instrument, a nose flute. Not in the least put out by our presence he continued to play, holding the flute to one nostril while blocking the other with his thumb. The last rays of sun enabled me to photograph him from all angles. Rouget was delighted at the idea of recording this music; the disc would probably be unique. The melody was simple, the tone muffled—in fact it was snuffling.

While we were making preparations to leave, another canoe arrived: in this was M. Chevallier, the Administrator of Lastoursville, who was used to touring his parish by river, which is the only means of communication between Franceville and Boué. Because of the rapids, only canoes can be used on the Ogowe, at least on the upper and middle reaches.

We set off lazily, accompanied by the Administrator, who moved from canoe to canoe chatting, intensely curious to know some of the details of our life among the Pygmies. The hours passed quickly, and very soon we came to the new rapids of Doumi. Our heaviest baggage had been put ashore, but in order to film the passage Trotty remained in the canoe in the middle of the boiling torrent. To the enormous pleasure of the crew he had fixed his black cameraman's hood at the end of a rod, delighting them with this magnificent dark flag.

Across the grey sky the heavy clouds loomed even darker. Far away in a village a hut was burning, trailing a long plume of smoke across the forest. The boatmen were in fine form now; we were in the heart of the Adouma country; it was a point of honour for the crews to race to be first at Lastoursville, and challenging cries rang from bank to bank of the river.

We waited forty-eight hours in this settlement, which had been founded by Brazza under the name of Madiville, the oil town, and where Rigail de Lastour had died of an attack of malaria. There was a block of granite on a slight rise which bore the simple epitaph "R. de Lastour, died here for France". Down below were the houses of the Administrator and the medical authorities, the offices, the hospital and the river superintendent. M. Chevallier had assembled all the populations of the neighbouring villages, and the whole of that day we filmed, recorded and photographed the dancers.

As the dust rose and glinted in the sunshine three drums, long and cone-shaped and held between the knees of the musicians, resounded under the fists and the drumsticks. The dance was one in which men and women shared. In the middle of the ring were two masked characters in the usual grotesque habiliments. One of them, the symbol of virility, was dressed in feathers, his face heavily charcoaled, enormously bearded with raffia, streaked and scrawled with broad white lines. The feminine symbol was also a man; a pierrot's face under a monkey-skin hat, grotesquely painted, somehow bearing two expressions at once: one of a celestial serenity, the other of a tormented carnal sensuality. They shuffled ritually, face to face, until the female symbol moved from the scene, leaving the male to execute a series of gambols, leaps and violent entrechats of the most sensational agility. Then he bounded off in pursuit of the female, a climax which sent the crowd into transports of amusement.

Rain again, and more rain; outside our door a relentless grey wall, and a muddy porridge underfoot. There had been nothing to do all day except play cards. I was staring through this soaking curtain when I saw approaching three silhouettes under an immense umbrella. I waved them over and they approached. I was astonished to see that they were three Pygmies, one of them a woman; they were Babinga Babongo. They crouched against the wall but they refused to come in. I made myself understood with gestures, enquiring where they had come from, and where they were going. They pointed with the umbrella vaguely down the road which crossed the settlement; there at the end of it began the forest.

Chapter XV

SO the canoe formation set off down the Ogowe
again, Patricio leading the singing with one of their
favourite airs, "Miseria Dia, Konga Miseria". *Miseria*
is a word borrowed from the Spanish and Portuguese
colonists, the first to arrive on this coast of Africa. The
canoe men associate it, not altogether unhappily, with
the difficulties of their own work; it is tremendously
exhausting paddling up the river, and sometimes peri-
lous in the rapids. We passed a group of fetish rocks in
the middle of this turbulent water: two great blocks on
the top of which a third was balanced. Aquatic plants
lie scattered round the base of this curious structure,
capped by the droppings of birds. The dying sun shone
on our face and prevented the cinema men from working. We stayed the night in the village of Maouya, on
the left bank—a double row of huts and a sandy beach
at the foot of an emerald-green hill.

The upper course of the Ogowe returned to its
original south–north direction. In the morning mist
we came to new rapids at Boundji, which were in high
flood. Before we nosed into this tormented grey water
Jean-Baptiste took a twig broom and sprinkled the surface of the river saying, "With canoes, we are the kings,

we are the strongest, the water tiger even does not frighten us."

It never proved possible to obtain an accurate description of this animal, the water tiger; it represents in their eyes all the spirits of the river, and it is in this way that they intercede for its favour.

Very soon we were sailing between soft, round hills covered with high grass; a red antelope covered the ground with fast, electric bounds; farther away in the undergrowth a buffalo ground his way among the branches.

We spent the night at Boumbakari, fighting a savage, useless war against the almost invisible insects which found no difficulty in penetrating the mesh of our mosquito-nets. Their bite was not infected with malaria, nor was there any danger of their transmitting sleeping-sickness: nevertheless, they provoked an almost insupportable irritation which made sleep completely out of the question, and it was a very tired crowd which embarked next morning for Kankan, at the junction of the Invindo and the Ogowe.

Squatting on our hard little seats, we could do no more than allow ourselves to be carried along, lulled by the endless singing of the boatmen. It was always the same melody, following a rhythm either slow or fast led by the cadence of the paddles.

Now a genuine problem presented itself, that of provisions; we were no longer in the Adouma country, and the ancestors of the Chaké, whose territory we were now in, had not always enjoyed very good relations with those of our boatmen. In spite of a lot of talk from Patricio our first stop had produced us nothing at all. We made an agreement that we would try more efficient methods, so at the next village, while we occupied the attention of the inhabitants, Dominique investigated a farmyard; in a little while four strong men were embarking two large sheep without anybody complaining. We paid very highly for them anyway.

At the union of the two rivers the black water became densely flecked with a thick, white froth; I had the agreeable impression of floating upon several square miles of Guinness. We had spent a splendid and peaceful evening at Kankan; it was one of those moments when everyone for some reason is delighted and rewarded in the company of everyone else, without calculation or thought, simply because the environment is propitious and everyone *is*, for the moment, without calculation or thought. We had already recorded Patricio; sitting beside us he continued to play his *sandzi* without consideration or vanity, partly for our pleasure but mostly for his own.

Before we got to Boué, the beginning of Mokandé territory, where we should have to change crews (because our men and the Badouma share the transport on the river), Patricio Mabouédi assembled us all on a tongue of sand in the shade of two great mango trees, of which the fruit was not yet ripe. Then, calling for silence, he said:

"The Badouma are strong, they are the kings of the boatmen. At Franceville we promised that the rapids would be passed, the machines for making pictures and the machines for making music would not have any water on them. We have paddled very hard, now we are very tired. Boué is not far now, before the sun goes down we want to celebrate. For us it is over, give us a good present and we shall be happy."

The approach to Boué was magnificent. The river flowed between hills that fell sharply towards the banks, but with rounded summits rolling towards the horizon, with lines of forest slicing across the green grass of the upper slopes. Under our eyes, a hundred yards farther on, was a monumental staircase of little cascades and excited water, falls and whirlpools, mist and spray, all dancing and bounding with an endless rumble. Huge tree trunks dragged there by the last flood rested somehow suspended in a precarious equilibrium over rocks polished like jet by centuries of angry water. No tribe of boatmen will risk them at this time of the year, the water is too violent.

The chief of the Okandé country, Auguste Moignon, brother—a colossal man with a terrible child's face on the shoulders of an athlete—and another chief crewman, called the "Boxer", came to offer their services. According to the Administrator the new boatmen would be even stronger and more adept than the old ones. But our discussion was interrupted by the sudden appearance of a local celebrity—he was a gay old man with white hair; on his chest he wore an ancient military medal; he came into the office, sat down without the slightest hesitation in the best chair, laid a hand on the box of cigarettes and filled his pockets as though by right. This, it turned out, was the old *boy* of M. Savorgnan de Brazza.

Organised by Auguste, brandishing an umbrella and wearing a magnificent black felt hat, we got under way eventually in spite of a great deal of emotional talk and physical excitement. The Mokandé canoes are very nearly identical with those of the Badouma, except they are perhaps a little longer and certainly lower: we could look forward to being drenched even more efficiently.

The bells began to ring, the songs to be sung, the flags to float, and we got away to an intensely dramatic start; there was the wildest competition to fling the canoes into action; we began our journey in a flurry of spray and loud excited cries. Once we were on the water the "pirates" seemed a little more tranquil, but the calm was only temporary, because they were soon contending all over again; challenges rang from canoe to canoe; the journey became a series of hundred-yard dashes.

But they were good, they were zealous, their superb arms and shoulders moved like clockwork; they seemed to pay no heed to the semi-visible rocks and the enormous floating trees, and yet at the last second they always managed to avoid them. Under their tremendous muscular urge the canoes seemed to achieve a certain elasticity, even a certain personal enthusiasm.

Dominique's canoe passed mine, Rouget's canoe passed his, they were all passed by the canoe of Auguste Moignon. Finally the cinema canoe detached itself from the rest and its boatmen became delirious with victory. Some of them threw their paddles in the air, others stood up and leaned over on all sides at the serious risk of overbalancing the fragile craft. Nobody, however, would confess himself beaten. The air still rang with vociferations of general triumph. Some people win canoe races but nobody ever loses them.

In practically no time we were at Achouka, an Okandé village with huts ranged along the river bank, where we disembarked our gear. It seemed a good idea to give a gun and some cartridges to one of the boatmen; if he could get a buffalo or two we should not be short of meat for some time.

PLATE 31. Death of an elephant: the Mokandé Africans of Achouka busy with the interminable butchery that follows the chase, everyone seeking the choicest parts.

PLATE 32. At Kongo-Boumba, among the Mokandé tribe: defying the sabre and the
jests of Okwi, the little boy moves in to the attack. Inch by inch, encouraged by the nearness
of his "supporter", he gains ground and then, finally, leaps between the legs of the Masked
Dancer.

At dusk, when I was helping Trotty to close up a film tin, a little child ran up crying excitedly, "Elephant, elephant!" As I followed him, running, he explained that the huntsman had found the trace of a solitary elephant that was going to drink at the river. He had tracked the animal down and was himself hiding in a clump of trees. When we got to the edge of the swamp I could see several dark figures, which turned out to be our boatmen. They advised me not to approach any nearer.

Then there was a rustling of branches, and underneath the bushes I saw the enormous shape of the elephant. Two bullets had already struck its spine, it was unable to charge. Another shot seemed to have no effect, yet another one provoked the most terrible clamour; the air rocked with something that reminded me of the trumpets of Jericho, ringing and terrible. The elephant had fallen on its knees, but it was not the end; slowly it rose again. But already the news had spread, and everyone in the neighbourhood was preparing to celebrate this windfall of a ton of meat so fortunately deposited on their doorsteps.

It was not till dawn that we returned there; Jacques and Trotty had brought their cameras. We approached the marsh, the huntsman loaded his gun—but there was no need: the elephant lay there stretched out under a cloud of flies and mosquitoes. It had died in the night. Its stomach was an enormous inflated balloon and its little eyes were closed. While we waited for the sun to rise, to begin our photography, the boatmen began impatiently sharpening their knives.

The man who had killed the elephant began by cutting off the tail and the trunk; those were the parts that belonged to him by right. With these things amputated and its enormous ears too, the king of the forest had a grotesque and pathetic appearance. Then they began to rid it of its inch-thick hide. The dismemberment was on an enormous scale, it took ten men to carry each joint.

The sun was afire, the air was stifling, the insects were insupportable. When Moignon struck his machete into the belly of the dead animal there came a terrible hiss and the whole cadaverous edifice collapsed, discharging a foetid smell. While the men marched around in a shambles of blood, tripe, urine and excrement, this monstrous butchery continued. There was meat for everybody; it seemed that the intestines were the most appreciated morsels. A small child began to dance with excitement; in the stomach he had found a little fish the elephant had swallowed the night before when it was refreshing itself at the river.

After they had copiously helped themselves, the boatmen distributed what was left to the villagers. They would smoke as much meat as they could to preserve it. and during the night the fires gleamed all around the huts. We ate the trunk that night for dinner; it is not as wonderful as some travellers allege—its taste is not unlike boiled beef, savourless and uninteresting. The tusks were of a good size; a doctor from Boué, who had come with us, took them away with him. We had a permit to kill three elephants. He alleged that we were on a reserve; nobody had told us that this was the case, but we saw no reason to argue.

We moved on again in canoes laden with elephant meat; for many days we were not to escape its smell. We had had a party with some unexpected aspects: the village had produced an accordionist well worthy of a Parisian Bal Musette, and it seemed there were many skilful waltzers. There had also been dancing more African—with *tutus* of raffia, head-dresses of feathers, painted bodies, hour after hour of precise and gracious movement.

After Boléko the Ogowe river becomes vast and broad and calm, and the canoes moved between banks of mangroves trailing their thousand roots in the flood. Then again there are rapids, a labyrinth of successive falls—we were not able to unload our gear, but the Mokandé knew the channels perfectly, standing up in the boats, their great poles in their hands; when it was calm they followed in line astern, when the waters became difficult each boatman chose the course he liked the best. There were times when the pole slipped on the glistening rocks, skidded, and suddenly we would be travelling down a liquid toboggan with the boatmen unable to do more than steer round obstacles as best they could, seeking a patch of still water where they might draw their breath.

Completely helpless, but nevertheless completely confident in the reflexes of our pilots, we abandoned ourselves to the strange and thrilling experience. Several times we were saved from capsizing only by the extraordinary dexterity of the crew; their bodies seemed to be an extension of their boat. Like the Badouma, the Mokandé always sing when the navigation does not occupy all their attention; but their tunes are livelier and more rhythmic than those of their neighbours; there are interminable litanies, called "Kombokomba", and songs in a rather higher key, called "Ipéga", or "Foumbéna", a sequence of responses and calls between the pilots and their crews.

We awoke, as usual, in the rain. Auguste Moignon had no great difficulty in persuading us to rest a little longer in Kongo-Boumba, though by the insistence of his manner we guessed that something was in the wind.

The Mokandé are given to unexpected bursts of activity. Today they assembled almost inconsequentially in the village centre, with the drummers lining up before a shelter in which sat two men, apparently dignitaries. A dozen or so urchins scampered around singing and beating bamboo wands together. It was a strange random symphony: the murmur of the drums, the rustling of the leaves, the endless shrill of the insects, the rise and fall of human conversation. After one or two experimental measures by the young people the "Boxer" arrived, wearing a brilliant loincloth. Then the uproar became deafening. Without any warning, Okwi leaped abruptly from the door of a hut hitherto tightly shut. For a moment the two remained face to face; the first man began a sequence of tight leaps from foot to foot, of whirls and arabesques imitated faithfully by the other. Okwi wore a head-dress of black and white plumes, a monkey-skin round the neck, a curious garb of plaited straw. His black face and brow, eyes and nose were picked out in staring white. The blank face and the sword with which he was armed contrasted with the delicacy of his waving head-dress and the gentle rustle of his movements. I could not take my eyes from him. Suddenly he threw himself towards the children, threatening them, miming an attack.

Meanwhile a lad of about twelve had joined the "Boxer" beside the drummers—just for a moment, because now the "Boxer" re-entered the ring; once again it seemed for a while as though one dancer mirrored the other. Then Okwi moved slowly towards the musicians;

their zeal became instantly multiplied, and Okwi flung himself into an intricate, exalted movement; he became a whirlwind. Suddenly he stopped, and the little boy entered, followed by the "Boxer", who knelt on the ground and seemed to be drawing strength from the earth. Okwi surrounded them, imprisoned them in movement, advanced on the supplicating figure and the boy. Inch by inch they retreated; the "Boxer", who in some fashion seemed to represent the boy's protector, rose and rejoined the dance. The sword whirled around him and the cane cut the air before his sweat-soaked face; nevertheless he attacked. The dance reversed itself again. The boy advanced, as though encouraged by the presence of his patron.

The symbolism seemed clear: the adolescent fighting for his place among his peers. He darted between the legs of Okwi, who instantly leaped back to bar his road. But the boy redoubled his assault, and triumphed over the straw man by vanishing into Okwi's house and barricading it. Okwi hurled himself against it, miming frustration and despair, and finally closed the sequence by bowing before the watching dignitaries.

The crowd faded away, the drums were removed, the women—to whom these ceremonies are forbidden—reappeared. This was the last ritual dance we were to see.

We went down to the river to bathe. The boatmen had lined up their craft on the bank and had lit great fires under them; protected by mud, they seemed to float in a pool of flames and writhing smoke, watched most carefully by the paddlers. The purpose, they said, was to make the hulls more waterproof and to rid them of insects.

Next day was the departure for Elarmakoura, then Ndjolé, and, on the Sunday night, under the storm clouds, the metalled road, an evil-tempered official, and the impossibility of finding a slice of bread. We had sailed two days without shelter in the rain; we were expected at Lambaréné. The rhythm of the paddles never changed; we were drenched; this was the Equator and our teeth were chattering. Even the boatmen shivered under their rags—why does no one sell these people waterproof coats and woollen jerseys, instead of trumpery trade-goods?

Louis said suddenly, "Very bad journey; canoes, black men, white men, all beaten."

The last seventy-five miles of the final stage were grim; the nearer we approached the coast, the more densely did the sky heap itself with impenetrable clouds. The banks widened all the time; on either side the forestry establishments grew more frequent. The boatmen's pace increased with the dusk; then we were in sight of Lambaréné. The town is on an island, we had to cut across the river to find the landing. A little swell met us on the beam, the waves broke against our canoes. In excellent order our flotilla came round the point, and it was already night when we reached the end of our journey.

Anthropology of the Pygmies

THE term *Pygmy* designates in general a group of peoples geographically separated from each other and having one common characteristic: a very small stature.

The fact that there have been Pygmies in Africa, in Asia, and in Oceania raises problems that are difficult to resolve. Does it suggest a common racial origin, associated with a common parentage? Are they wholly independent of each other, with their small size merely a matter of coincidence? Are they, or are they not, a primitive race? Could it be that the Pygmies are a simple development, or degeneration, of the ordinary African? If none of these—who are they, and where do they come from?

Before attempting to answer these questions, it will be helpful to define, briefly, the Pygmies of Africa, since it is with them that this book concerns itself.

The African Pygmies are *Negrillos*. Living almost entirely apart from the Africans, and having with them only tenuous associations of trade—or rather, barter—they are a nomad people living by the chase and by the gathering of wild crops in a strictly limited area: the Equatorial Forest. They practise neither grazing nor agriculture, they do not understand the crafts of metalwork or pottery, they have a merely rudimentary civilisation with a cultural peak similar to that of the Stone Age men.

White observers have examined them often; our own researches generally confirm the conclusions of other ethnographers and anthropologists.

Their habitat is bounded by the Equatorial forest-band, extending from west to east and involving the Gabon, the Cameroons, the French and Belgian Congoes, and South Oubangi. Outside this zone there are no Pygmies. Within it their groupings are very sparse and their communities small. It is very imprecisely assessed that the greatest number of their camps is in the Belgian Congo.

They are nomads, however, moving freely between territories, and they have avoided every census; thus the estimates of their population vary from authority to authority.

One can consider as authentic the following: A major group, the Bambouti (and kindred forms) of the Belgian Congo, are the smallest of the African Pygmies; they are a pure race numbering about 25,000. A second group is that of the Babinga of the Gabon, the Cameroons, the French Congo and the South of Oubangi; they are mostly pure-blood, but their number is indeterminable—25 to 30,000. Then there are the Batoua of the Congo, less pure and consequently a little bigger, owing to miscegenation. These are Pygmoids rather than Pygmies, and there are about 50,000 of them. It seems possible that there are about 100,000 African Pygmies all told.

The Negrillos of Overseas France are essentially represented by the Babinga, who constitute a sub-race, in the biological sense. That is, they are defined by a certain standard of anatomical, physiological and pathological characteristics. It is the examination of biological characteristics that constitutes anthropology. It is true that one must go further and define anthropology as something that depends on a broad analysis; the average is what is important; the scientists eliminate the "individual variation".

What are the racial characteristics of the Babinga? The average stature is always below five feet and, in the camps we saw, oscillates around four feet seven inches, for the males. The pigmentation is sometimes black, sometimes red-brown, sometimes *café-au-lait*. They are more hirsute than the other Africans; many Pygmies grow a strong beard and have a certain hairy development on the chest. The skull is shorter and rounder than the African's (sometimes slightly dolichocephalic or brachycephalic, but usually mesocephalic). The lips are relatively thin. The chin retreats only slightly. The nose is disproportionately big, with well-developed nostrils, having the form of an equilateral triangle. The very acute eyes exhibit, in a third of cases, the shape known as "mongolian", slightly slanting, with a folded upper eyelid. Curiously, the size of head is normal; the Pygmy's is proportionately highly developed in comparison with the body. The legs are short and the arms are long—precisely the opposite of what one generally sees among Negroes.

These characteristics prevent one from considering the Pygmies as miniature Negroes: the shape of the cranium, the thinner lips, the larger nose, the shape of the eye, the asymmetric head, the proportions of the trunk and limbs and the hairiness, all indicate a separate race.

The following customs are also distinctive: the head is shaved in both sexes, with the exception of an occasional tuft or topknot; the boys are circumcised; the face is lightly tattooed with blue lines; the lobe of the right ear is perforated, sometimes also the upper lip; the teeth are sometimes filed to a point.

Physiologically also, the Pygmy differs in many respects from the Negro: a thyroid gland both smaller and less active; a slower heart-beat; sebaceous glands secreting a substance of unusual composition with a strong smell. The blood-groups suggest a classification different from the Negroes, who belong more to Group O (universal donors); the Pygmies are mainly A and B.

The Pygmy reaction to sickness is also different. The Pygmy has a good resistance to local pathological factors: in spite of the abundance of the tsetse fly, sleeping-sickness does not affect him; he has developed a certain immunity to malaria. Other diseases that attack the local Negro—syphilis, leprosy, tuberculosis—find him apparently resistant.

The high rate of reproduction in each family easily compensates for the heavy figures of infant mortality due to malaria and rickets resulting from the insufficiency of violet-rays in the depths of the forest. Apart from the numerous accidents met with while hunting, the Pygmies seem fairly long-lived, a number being over 70 years old, and the principal cause of death is probably hypertension brought on by a diet consisting almost exclusively of meat.

Apart from racial traits, the Negrillos differ radically from the Negroes in a series of ethnographic characteristics (domestic, social, juridical and religious) which correspond to a strict conditioning to a nomadic life in a dense forest. They are monogamous, where the Negroes are in general polygamous (which is explained partly by the influence of imported religions and is also to a degree associated with agriculture and breeding). They live in highly coherent small communities, separated by great distances, uniting for political reasons of which the most important is co-ordinating the hunting. They are monotheistic in a country largely polytheistic (where Islam has not penetrated).

The Pygmy, small though he is, is remarkably well physically adapted to his surroundings; he is not a degenerate; his smallness is the consequence of a feeble, though not pathological, functioning of the thyroid gland. He has an evolved culture (music, legends, mythology). His material civilisation has remained archaic only because he has always lived on the fringe of world cultural currents, where the only possible life could revolve round the chase.

We have said that Pygmies exist elsewhere—the Negrito of the Andaman Islands, the Vedda of Ceylon and South India, the Semang of Malacca, the Aeta of the Philippines. They have, however, nothing in common with the Negrillo except their small stature. One cannot talk biologically of a "Pygmy group".

No definite hypothesis has been arrived at regarding the origins of the African Negrillos. It could be that they were there before the Negroes, and were then dispersed and decimated and forced to take refuge in the dense forest. Their hyperthyroid character, the mongolian eye, their long hair, their blood groups, all suggest that they are relics of ancient immigrations from the North-East, from Asia, and that in fact the Negrillos are the vestigial trace of an ancient yellow-African stock, to be considered with other small races like the Hottentots and Bushmen of South Africa.

RAOUL HARTWEG

Results of the Ogowe-Congo Mission

THE ethnographic researches of our expedition were made mostly among the Babinga Babenzélé and the Bangombé Pygmies, as well as among the neighbouring African communities, the Pomo and Ngoundi. A hundred articles of scientific value have been deposited in the Musée de l'Homme, some of them displayed in the case devoted to Negrillos.

The anthropological work with the Babinga consisted of:

(*a*) measurement;

(*b*) a study of the blood-groups, the demographic and sanitary conditions;

(*c*) consideration of bodily mutilations and dental characteristics.

Following a different route, the Prehistory group undertook an extensive exploration of the Mayam region, prospecting also in the valleys of the Nyari and the Nyanga. Nearly two thousand prehistoric stonework objects were also deposited in the Musée de l'Homme, in the Prehistoric Department.

Three documentary films were completed, entitled: "Congo Dances", "In the Land of the Pygmies", and "Canoes on the Ogowe", for the Société d'Applications Cinématographiques (S.D.A.C.).

A collection of five hundred and forty sides of discs were recorded among seventeen communities in the

Middle Congo, eight riverine tribes of the Ogowe, and two Babinga groups. In addition to the sound track of the films, the recordings were edited on discs, with explanatory notes, as follows:

Musée de l'Homme (Paris): 34 discs (78 r.p.m., 29 of 25 cm. [10 ins.] and 5 of 30 cm. [12 ins.]);
La Boîte à Musique (Paris): 3 discs (78 r.p.m., 30 cm.);
Pathé (Paris): 3 discs (78 r.p.m., 25 cm.);
Ethnic Folkways Library (New York): 4 discs (78 r.p.m., 25 cm.);
Columbia (New York), on LP;
U.N.E.S.C.O., "Universal Collection of Popular Recorded Music": 1 disc (78 r.p.m., 25 cm.).

This collection, without pretending to be definitive, nevertheless presents a relatively extensive picture of the peoples encountered, particularly the Babinga Pygmies.